GUY'S GUIDE

TO

EATING WELL

A MAN'S COOKBOOK FOR HEALTH AND WELLNESS

HOLLY CLEGG AND CURTIS CHASTAIN, MD

Holly Clegg

© 2018 by Holly Clegg
Photographs © 2018 by Holly Clegg and Lee Jackson

Library of Congress Control Number: 2017918073

ISBN-13 978-0-9996265-0-4

Cover and composition by Rikki Campbell Ogden / pixiedesign
Cover illustration by Jonathan Fenske
Edited by Lee Jackson, LDN, RD
Nutritional analysis by Tammi Hancock, Hancock Nutrition

Available books by Holly Clegg:
  Eating Well Through Cancer
  Eating Well To Fight Arthritis
  Holly Clegg's trim&TERRIFIC® KITCHEN 101
  Holly Clegg's trim&TERRIFIC® Too Hot in the Kitchen
  Holly Clegg's trim&TERRIFIC® Gulf Coast Favorites
  Holly Clegg's trim&TERRIFIC® Diabetic Cooking
  Alimentándose bien durante el cáncer

Production and Manufacturing
Favorite Recipes Press
An imprint of
FRP
P.O. Box 305142
Nashville, TN 37230
800-358-0560

On the front cover:
Chicken with Tomato Topping and Mozzarella, pg. 33

On the back cover:
Grilled Shrimp Margherita Pizza, pg. 171
Tuna Tacos with Wasabi Cream and Mango Salsa, pg. 56
Beef Fajitas in Slow Cooker, pg. 162

Printed in China

CONTENTS

ACKNOWLEDGEMENTS

I always say, things in life happen for a reason. As a devoted caregiver and daddy's girl, while I finalized this book, my father lost his long-courageous battle with cancer and heart disease. I am humbled and honored to dedicate this book to him. Throughout his life he showed us all how to fight for your health and win.

When I think about who to acknowledge for this book, I couldn't have made it through this year without my deep support system. My father left behind my mother, Ruth, who embodies strength and inspiration with their beautiful marriage of 65 years. My power team of my devoted husband, Mike, of 38 years and all our incredible, caring children and their spouses, Todd and Sana, Courtney and Chad, and Haley and Eric. Mae Mae, my Baton Rouge mother and #1 taste tester. My sister and brother, Ilene and Michael, whom I treasure our unbreakable bond. My right and left hand, Lee, my dietician, who has been with me for over 10 years. To my friends who are family, the Stephens, Bombets, Hansbroughs, both Goldbergs, Dagermans, Rothschilds, Rosenblooms, Kraines, Michele, Melanie and Pam, my sister-in-law.

Last but not least. To all of you out there, thank you for continuing to support me on my journey and bringing health and wellness to your homes!

–HOLLY CLEGG

I am thankful to each and every one of you who have given me the opportunity to participate in your healthcare; your trust and loyalty mean everything to me. I am committed to continue to provide you with the best medical care available for as long as I practice medicine.

I thank my wife Chanel for being such a great listener, and for being my biggest fan and best friend. She has always supported me in every endeavor I have undertaken. I am so proud of our incredible children, Kati, Curtis, Ashley, and Julianne, and I thank them for always being so proud of me.

While many of my medical skills have been developed during my years of practicing medicine, two physicians were responsible for mentoring me, and training me to be the physician I am today. To these men I am forever grateful: Dr. Ronald B. George and Dr. Donald T. Erwin.

I would like to acknowledge the late Robert C. Davidge, former CEO of Our Lady of the Lake Hospital for supporting my vision of creating my unique Men's Health practice.

Thanks to my parents, Rodney and Joan Chastain for the sacrifices they made to make sure I received the best education possible to prepare me for medical school.

Finally, thanks to Holly Clegg for inviting me to be her partner in this incredible project. Her tireless energy and commitment to healthy cooking and healthy living resonates perfectly with my passion for medicine.

–CURTIS CHASTAIN, MD

A NOTE FROM HOLLY

Men! I have a husband, son, brother, and grandson, so guys and food are on my radar! We know you cook for different reasons: relaxation, necessity, or you have to grill. But, what about cooking for your health? How do you keep a healthy heart or get control of your diet when you find yourself at a sports bar surrounded by beer and burgers?

As a healthy culinary expert who has sold over 1.5 million easy healthy cookbooks, I decided the men in my life could use some assistance in the kitchen. The newest edition to my *Eating Well* series, *Guy's Guide To Eating Well*, focuses on men's health and wellness to guide men (or their significant others) in the kitchen.

I am thrilled to partner with Dr. Curtis Chastain, a physician who specializes in men's wellness. Together, we will give you the tools to eat better helping prevent and control diabetes, heart disease, cancer, obesity, joint pain and even address testosterone troubles for a better lifestyle. Don't worry, our recipes go beyond health. We created chapters based on the busy man or even the outdoor expert.

Think of this men's cookbook as your wellness bible packed with simple recipes, reference information, and terrific tips to keep you and those surrounding you healthy. This book is for men, women, and families. Health doesn't discriminate.

 Freezer-friendly recipes that you can make ahead

 Vegetarian recipes

 Gluten-free recipes

 Diabetic-friendly recipes that meet ADA guidelines

Each recipe includes the nutritional analysis and the diabetic exchange. The analysis is based on the larger servings. The nutritional analysis does not include any salt or pepper (since it is listed to taste) or any ingredient with "optional" after it.

Chicken Pesto Pasta **PAGE 50**

PREFACE
THE PREVENTIVE HEALTH CONCEPT

BY CURTIS CHASTAIN, MD

I started practicing medicine in 1990. During my training as an Internal Medicine physician and in subsequent years, I learned how to diagnose and manage very sick patients. In fact, the more complex the patient was, the more I liked taking care of them. And then one day in the Emergency room, my perspective on medicine changed forever.

I was called to the ER to admit a 54 year old man having a heart attack. The patient was new to me. There is a lot of activity that goes on during a heart attack evaluation - lots of beeping noises, blinking lights and people moving really quickly.

I examined my new patient while the nursing staff was inserting IV's and drawing requisite labwork. I began thumbing through his chart and I quickly learned that he had a history of uncontrolled high blood pressure, high cholesterol; he was a smoker, and his father had a heart attack early in life. All of these are risk factors for the very event he was suffering from at that very moment.

There was a tap on my shoulder; the patient's wife wanted to speak with me about her husband's condition. I stepped out of the small room into the hallway and introduced myself to the patient's wife and young son. She was weeping and trying to gather her thoughts. And then she asked me the question that changed the way I practiced medicine forever. She asked, "Doctor, how could this happen?"

I realized at that moment that I could either tell her a lie, "Ms. Smith, I have no idea how this could have happened, you know—bad things just happen to good people sometimes. Nobody could have seen this coming." Or, I could tell her the truth.... "Ms. Smith, I hate to tell you this, but anyone could have seen this coming 10 years ago, and your husband may die today because he never took the time to take care of himself.

THOUGHTS ON PREVENTIVE MEDICINE

Medical training teaches physicians how to take care of sick people, and that's a good thing because when you're sick, you need a physician who is trained to treat your particular disease. But what if your goal is to prevent getting sick and/or reducing your chances of dying from disease in the first place?

Disease Prevention, or more appropriately, "Death prevention" is an evolving area of medicine that I have found to very professionally rewarding. Although my "disease treating skills" are still alive and well, why not use my "medical detective skills" to find the guy who is "supposed to" have a heart attack, or the guy who is "supposed to" die from cancer, and then help prevent either one of them from happening?

You see, you and I are playing the same game—it's called "Let's live as long as we're supposed to," otherwise known as "Longevity." As you will see, the threats to longevity are few, and relatively easy to identify. These threats can be invariably neutralized, which increases the odds of reaching longevity.

We all have our appointed day to leave this world, and I'm sure most of you feel the same way I do—I love my family and my life so much, I would prefer to live until my appointed day with the best health possible.

Unfortunately, it isn't that easy. There are 4 basic threats to longevity. They are: 1) a cardiovascular event, 2) cancer, 3) an accident, and 4) other. I'll take them one at a time and break them down for you.

Other

We're talking about diseases that nobody can anticipate like, Alzheimer's, or Lou Gerhig's disease, or some other life shortening devastating disease. If you can't anticipate it, you can't prevent it, so let's throw that out.

Accident

An accident is also an unanticipated event; nobody can predict being hit by a car, or falling off a ladder, so let's throw that one out too.

So now we're down to two threats to longevity, cardiovascular disease and cancer. And if you're not one, by default you have to be the other. If you could figure out which one of the two diseases threatens you most, wouldn't you do everything you could to protect yourself against that threat? Truth is, you already do this in your home and business lives every day, and you don't even think about it; it's called profiling.

Cardiovascular Disease

Cardiovascular disease comes in two flavors: heart attack and stroke. A heart attack is death to heart muscle and a stroke involves death to brain tissue. Both diseases for the most part are a result of blockage in blood vessels from cholesterol plaque, a condition known as atherosclerotic cardiovascular disease (ASCVD).

Risk factors for ASCVD are well known:
- Family history of ASCVD
- High blood pressure
- High cholesterol
- Diabetes
- Obesity
- Tobacco use
- Sedentary lifestyle

So if your father had a heart attack, and his father had a heart attack, guess what? You're probably in line for a heart attack! Similarly, if you have any or all of the risk factors above, the likelihood is high that at some point, your life is going to be dramatically interrupted by a heart attack or a stroke.

Cancer

Approximately 70% of all male cancer deaths are caused by only four cancers:
- Colon cancer
- Lung cancer
- Prostate cancer
- Skin cancer

Genetics plays a strong role in each of these cancers. So if one of your family members (father, mother, brother or sister) suffered or died from one of these cancers, you are at increased risk for that cancer.

HOW CAN I FIGURE IT OUT?

The answer to this question requires four basic steps.
- Find a doctor or mid-level provider
- Have routine blood tests done
- Schedule appropriate screening tests for cancer
- Get vaccinated

Find a Doctor

It is very important to find someone whom you can trust to profile your medical risk. It needs to be someone with whom you can communicate easily and someone whom you feel is trustworthy and who is also well educated. There are plenty of online sites to check out physicians' and mid-levels' background and training. Finally, ask friends and family for recommendations.

Routine Blood Tests

At a minimum, in order to properly profile an individual for the threat of ASCVD or Cancer, the following blood tests are necessary:
- **Complete Blood Count (CBC)**—checks for leukemia, low blood counts (anemia) and immune system.
- **Chemistry Panel**—identifies diabetes, and diseases that affect the liver, and kidneys.
- **Lipid Panel**—This test is necessary to identify whether you have high cholesterol. The results of this test can actually be used along with other test results to predict your risk of dying from a heart attack within the next 10 years.
- **PSA**—this is a very controversial screening test for prostate cancer, the second leading cause of cancer death in men.

- **TSH**—This blood test identifies whether the thyroid gland might be over or under active.
- **Urinalysis**—Screens for abnormal presence of blood, white cells, or protein which may indicate severe problems.

Screening Tests for Cancer

There are screening tests for the most common cancers in men. They are:

- **Chest x-ray**—used to identify lung cancer.
- **Colonoscopy**—used to identify early colon cancer or pre-cancerous polyps
- **Skin Exam**—performed by your medical provider to look for possible skin cancer. This should be done while you are completely disrobed.
- **Prostate Exam**—this is the test no man wants to have, but having this screening test may identify an early, very treatable prostate tumor.

Get Vaccinated

The mortality rate of community-acquired pneumonia remains high, despite all of the antibiotic therapy available to us as medical providers. One of the best ways to prevent death from pneumonia is by becoming vaccinated. While you're at it, make sure you are up to date on your tetanus vaccine as well. If you're over 60, you're in line for a shingles vaccine as well.

SUMMARY

There is ongoing debate about whether cardiovascular disease and cancer are preventable. Could it be that some of us are destined to get one or the other no matter what is done to prevent it?

My thought is this: You may not be able to prevent yourself from getting ASCVD or cancer, but using the resources that are readily available, dying prematurely from either one of these two diseases can be prevented.

Grilled Shrimp Margherita Pizza **PAGE 171**

Baked Shrimp Scampi **PAGE 36**

FATIGUE

FATIGUE
WHY AM I SO DANG TIRED ALL THE TIME?

WHAT CAN CAUSE CHRONIC FATIGUE?
WHAT CAN I DO TO GET MY ENERGY BACK?
COULD I HAVE TESTOSTERONE DEFICIENCY?

Fatigue can affect almost every aspect of a man's life, and can be associated with many medical conditions from obesity to depression. I don't have an exact figure, but a recent study suggests the economic impact of chronic fatigue is in the hundreds of millions annually.

I wish I had a dollar for every time I've heard a story like the one below, not only in my medical practice, but also when I'm out in social settings. It seems that chronic tiredness is becoming an epidemic among males in the US, responsible for 5–7% of the complaints of men seeking medical treatment.

Joe Smith has been working in an Industrial Contracting company for the past 15 years. He is one of the top salesmen in the company, responsible for over $2.1M in sales annually. Recently, Joe was recognized by the company for his successes by being promoted to Regional Sales Manager. With the promotion came a significant increase in pay, and also a substantial increase in responsibility.

I saw Joe not long after his promotion; his main complaint was "feeling more tired than usual." He told me, "Doc, I used to get home and work in my shop or work in the yard. Now when I get home, all I want to do is sit on the couch and watch TV. I used to like fish, but when the weekends come, I just don't feel like doing anything. And one more thing Doc, I just haven't been myself in the bedroom. My wife is starting to think there's something wrong with me.

Here are more of the most common causes of chronic fatigue that I see in my practice.

- **Sleep disturbance.** The typical scenario is that a man can fall asleep, but he wakes up after 2-3 hours and cannot get back to sleep. This can be due to increased stressors in the workplace or at home, many times completely unrealized by the patient. Treatment depends on the cause of stress in a particular individual.

- **Poor dietary habits.** Men are notorious for skipping breakfast, eating a light to medium "healthy" lunch, and then consuming a massive supper full of calories. Energy comes from calories found in the proper foods that should be consumed throughout the day. Without proper food, there is no energy. Without energy, there is tiredness. Treatment involves dietary modification using proper meals consumed at proper intervals throughout the day to keep energy levels high.

- **Testosterone deficiency.** This is the least common cause of fatigue, but one that should not be overlooked. A testosterone deficient male is typically overweight, fatigued, and apathetic about the things that used to bring him happiness. The diagnosis is made by drawing blood for testosterone levels. Less than 10% of guys who come to my office with "fatigue" actually have testosterone deficiency.

Fatigue

Feeling sluggish? Are you the person that's grabbing for one of those energy drinks or frantically reaching for a caffeinated drink to give you that quick energy boost? Go a different route and maximize your energy by eating a balanced diet, of complex carbohydrates, protein, and unsaturated fats. Consider good nutrition the fuel that helps keep your energy levels up throughout the day, keeping fatigue at bay. Also, don't forget about snacks or smaller nutrition-rich meals, full of the correct macronutrients, help prevent blood sugar dips which promote fatigue. And be sure to stay hydrated to prevent feeling sluggish. When it comes to getting a good night sleep, try to avoid heavy meals, caffeine and alcohol right before going to sleep.

Energy Providing Macronutrients

Carbohydrates—Carbohydrate is the body's main source of fuel, easily used by the body as energy. Get the most nutrients and fiber to achieve a healthy weight and optimal energy by choosing complex carbohydrates over simple sugars for that slow burning effect without the big energy crash.

Complex Carbohydrate Food Choices:

- Whole grains: oats, brown rice, whole grain pasta
- Fruits and Vegetables
- Beans and Legumes

Protein—Protein is necessary to maintain muscle mass as well as transporting hormones and vitamins throughout the body. Protein also helps to repair body tissue and maintain a healthy immune system. Without enough protein, the body can take longer to recover from illness and you can have a lower resistance to infection. Protein in food breaks down into amino acids in the body which are the building blocks of protein. Nine essential amino acids cannot be made by the body and must come from food. There are eleven nonessential amino acids that can be made by the body and not necessary from diet.

Lean Protein Food Choices

- Eggs
- Meat
- Poultry
- Fish
- Low fat dairy products
- Nuts
- Beans
- Nuts
- Soy

Fat—Fats are a concentrated source of energy, meaning more calories per gram than other macronutrients, which can lead to weight gain if eaten too much. However, they are also essential for healthy body functions and development. Healthy unsaturated fats help your body to absorb and use vitamins, as well as helping to maintain cell membranes and lower "bad" LDL cholesterol.

Unsaturated Fat Food Choices:

- Oils: olive, canola, avocado
- Nuts: almonds, cashews, pecans, peanut butter, walnuts
- Fish: salmon, tuna
- Flaxseed
- Sesame seeds

BREAKFAST ENGLISH MUFFINS ON THE GO

Forget the drive through and grab this all-around nutrient-dense, quick breakfast when you're on-the-go. Western omelet ingredients piled on an English muffin—a fast favorite.

MAKES: 6 muffins · **PREP TIME:** 5 minutes · **COOK TIME:** 10 minutes ·

1/2 cup chopped Canadian bacon

1/4 cup chopped onion

1/4 cup chopped green bell pepper

1/3 cup chopped tomatoes

2 eggs

5 egg whites

Salt and pepper to taste

3 whole-wheat English muffins, halved

1/4 cup shredded reduced-fat Cheddar cheese

1 In nonstick skillet coated with nonstick cooking spray, cook Canadian bacon 2 minutes or until begins to brown. Add onion and green pepper sautéing until tender. Add tomatoes, cook 1 minute. Remove from pan, set aside.

2 In small bowl, whisk together eggs and egg whites. In same nonstick skillet coated with nonstick cooking spray, scramble eggs. Season to taste. When eggs are almost done, stir in bacon onion mixture.

3 Meanwhile, toast muffin halves. Divide egg mixture to top muffin halves. Sprinkle with cheese.

Prepared muffins may be refrigerated and reheated in microwave or in preheated oven 350°F about 5 minutes or until well heated.

Egg beaters may be substituted for egg and egg white combination.

NUTRITIONAL INFORMATION Calories 143 kcal, Calories from Fat 25%, Fat 4 g, Saturated Fat 1 g, Cholesterol 71 mg, Sodium 391 mg, Carbohydrates 15 g, Dietary Fiber 3 g, Total Sugars 4 g, Protein 12 g

DIETARY EXCHANGES 1 starch, 1 1/2 lean meat

GRILLADES

A man's meat-eater, Southern brunch with hearty seasoned
round steak cooked in rich brown gravy served over cheese grits.

MAKES: 8 (1-cup) servings · PREP TIME: 20 minutes · COOK TIME: 2 hours ·

2 pounds lean, boneless, beef round
   steak, trimmed and cut into 1-inch
   strips

Salt and pepper to taste

4 tablespoons all-purpose flour,
   divided

1 onion, chopped

1 green bell pepper, cored and
   chopped

1/2 cup chopped celery

1 1/2 cups chopped tomatoes (drained
   canned tomatoes may be used)

1 teaspoon minced garlic

2 cups fat-free beef broth

1 tablespoon cider vinegar

1 teaspoon dried thyme leaves

1 tablespoon Worcestershire sauce

1 bunch green onions, chopped

1 Season meat to taste and coat with 3 tablespoons of flour, shaking off excess.

2 In large nonstick skillet coated with nonstick cooking spray, brown meat over medium heat 5–7 minutes on each side. Remove from skillet and set aside.

3 To same skillet, add onion, bell pepper, celery, and tomatoes and cook over medium heat 5–7 minutes, stirring occasionally. Gradually add remaining 1 tablespoon flour, stirring one minute. Add garlic, broth, vinegar, thyme, and Worcestershire sauce, bring to boil.

4 Return meat to skillet. Reduce heat and cook, covered, 1 1/2 hours, or until meat is very tender, stirring occasionally. Sprinkle with green onions.

SERVING SUGGESTION

*Serve over Cheese Grits
(page 6) or rice.*

NUTRITION NUGGET

*Beef is one of the most complete
sources of high quality protein,
rich in all 9 essential amino
acids—helping promote muscle
maintenance and growth.*

NUTRITIONAL INFORMATION Calories 175, Calories from Fat 19%, Fat 4 g, Saturated Fat 1 g, Cholesterol 57 mg, Sodium 287 mg, Carbohydrates 9 g, Dietary Fiber 2 g, Total Sugars 4 g, Protein 25 g

DIETARY EXCHANGES 1 vegetable, 3 lean meat

CHEESE GRITS

Never had grits? Creamy cheesy grits, a Southern staple, pair well with
just about anything, from breakfast to savory meats.

MAKES: 8 (3/4-cup) servings · PREP TIME: 5 minutes · COOK TIME: 10 minutes ·

2 cups fat-free chicken broth

2 cups skim milk

1 cup water

1 1/2 cups quick grits

1 1/2 cups shredded reduced-fat
  sharp Cheddar cheese (more
  if desired)

2 teaspoons Worcestershire sauce

Salt and pepper to taste

Dash cayenne pepper

1 In medium pot, bring broth, milk, and water to boil. Add grits, reduce heat, cover, and cook about 5 minutes, or until grits are thickened and creamy.

2 Add remaining ingredients, stirring until cheese is melted. Serve immediately.

*Grits are made when corn
kernels are ground into course
meal, providing energy in the
form of complex carbohydrate.*

NUTRITIONAL INFORMATION Calories 200, Calories from fat 21%, Fat 5 g, Saturated Fat 3 g, Cholesterol 12 mg, Sodium 428 mg, Carbohydrate 27 g, Dietary Fiber 1, Sugars 4 g, Protein 11 g

DIABETIC EXCHANGES 2 starch, 1 lean meat

MEXICAN BREAKFAST CASSEROLE

Outrageously delicious and simple, this make-ahead "stick to your ribs" breakfast with eggs combined with tortillas, sausage, beans and southwestern flavors is a great way to start your day—or really any time of the day!

MAKES: 8–10 servings · PREP TIME: 15 minutes + refrigeration time · COOK TIME: 40–50 minutes ·

1 cup diced chicken sausage

1 (15-ounce) can black beans, drained and rinsed

1 (14-ounce) can tomatoes and green chilies, drained

1 bunch green onions, chopped

4 eggs

6 egg whites

2 cups fat-free half-and-half

2 teaspoons chili powder

6 (8-inch) corn tortillas, quartered

1 1/2 cups shredded reduced-fat Mexican-blend cheese

1 Coat 13×9×2-inch baking dish with nonstick cooking spray.

2 In small nonstick skillet, cook sausage until lightly browned, stirring, about 5 minutes. In bowl, combine sausage, black beans, tomatoes and green chilies, and green onions; set aside

3 In another bowl, whisk together eggs, egg whites, half-and-half and chili powder.

4 Spoon about 1/2 cup sausage mixture on bottom of prepared dish. Top with three tortillas, half the sausage mixture, half the cheese and repeat layers. Pour egg mixture evenly over casserole and refrigerate, covered, at least 6 hours or overnight.

5 Preheat oven 350°F. Bake 40–50 minutes or until bubbly and golden brown and knife inserted into custard comes out clean.

Put ingredients together the night before and pop in oven the next morning for an easy, amazing breakfast.

If using glass baking dish, place in cold oven.

Eggs are often considered the perfect protein because they contain the best quality and ratio of the body's 9 essential amino acids.

NUTRITIONAL INFORMATION Calories 258, Calories from Fat 25%, Fat 7 g, Saturated Fat 3 g, Cholesterol 97 mg, Sodium 800 mg, Carbohydrates 30 g, Dietary Fiber 4 g, Total Sugars 4 g, Protein 20 g

DIETARY EXCHANGES 2 starch, 2 lean meat

PEANUT BUTTER MIX

A homerun three-ingredient combination of complex carbs, protein and fat—honey and peanut butter make this tasty, sweet and salty snack a great solution to keep on hand when your energy dips.

MAKES: 6 (1/2-cup) servings · PREP TIME: 5 minutes · COOK TIME: 1 1/2 hours ·

2 tablespoons honey

3 tablespoons peanut butter

3 cups cereal (assorted shredded wheat, oatmeal chex, corn bran chex)

1 Preheat oven 175°F. Line baking pan with foil coated with nonstick cooking spray.

2 In microwave-safe dish, microwave honey and peanut butter about 20 seconds or until smooth. Toss with cereal, coating well. Spread on prepared baking pan. Bake 1 1/2 hours. Cool

You can also toss in your favorite nuts or dried fruit.

Peanut butter provides a good mix of healthy protein, unsaturated fat and carbohydrates for energy. Look for unprocessed versions of peanut butter for the lowest sugar and hydrogenated fat content.

NUTRITIONAL INFORMATION Calories 148, Calories from Fat 25%, Fat 4 g, Saturated Fat 1 g, Cholesterol 0 mg, Sodium 77 mg, Carbohydrates 26 g, Dietary Fiber 3 g, Total Sugars 7 g, Protein 4 g
DIETARY EXCHANGES 1 1/2 starch, 1/2 other carbohydrate, 1/2 fat

MEATY BISCUIT CUPS

An easy, all-star meal or snack of scrumptious Sloppy Joe-style meaty mixture
in a flaky crust is a real energy booster.

MAKES: 20 biscuit cups · **PREP TIME:** 15 minutes · **COOK TIME:** 10 minutes ·

---

1 pound ground sirloin

1/3 cup finely chopped red onion

1/3 cup barbecue sauce

1/2 cup frozen corn, thawed

1 (10-ounce) can flaky refrigerator biscuits

1/2 cup shredded reduced-fat sharp Cheddar cheese

1 Preheat oven 400°F. Coat muffin tins with nonstick cooking spray.

2 In medium nonstick skillet, cook meat and onion about 5 minutes or until meat is done, stirring occasionally. Drain any excess fat. Add barbecue sauce and corn, mixing well.

3 Split each biscuit in half and press each half into prepared tin. Press sides of each biscuit gently up into a cup shape.

4 Divide meat mixture into each biscuit cup and bake 10 minutes. Remove from oven and sprinkle with cheese immediately.

NUTRITION NUGGET

Ensure you are choosing the leanest cuts of meat by looking for those ending in "loin" or "round." Ground turkey may be used for ground sirloin.

SERVING SUGGESTION

Serve as filling afternoon snack or pair with roasted veggies or soup for a delectable meal.

NUTRITIONAL INFORMATION Calories 86, Calories from Fat 27%, Fat 3 g, Saturated Fat 1 g, Cholesterol 14 mg, Sodium 186 mg, Carbohydrates 9 g, Dietary Fiber 0 g, Total Sugars 3 g, Protein 7 g

DIETARY EXCHANGES 1/2 starch, 1 lean meat

BUFFALO CHICKEN DIP

What man doesn't like Buffalo wings? Forget the bars and make this simple-to-make, delicious dip with Buffalo wing-flavor for your men's night out at home.

MAKES: 24 (2-tablespoon) servings · **PREP TIME:** 5 minutes · **COOK TIME:** 10 minutes ·

---

1 (8-ounce) package reduced-fat cream cheese

1/2 cup shredded part-skim mozzarella cheese

1/2 cup hot sauce or Buffalo Wing sauce

1 tablespoon dry Ranch Dressing mix

1/2 cup nonfat plain Greek yogurt

2 cups shredded cooked chicken breasts (rotisserie), skin removed

1 In medium nonstick pot, combine cream cheese, mozzarella cheese, hot sauce, and Ranch Dressing mix, stirring constantly, until mixture is creamy, about 5 minutes.

2 Add yogurt and chicken. Do not boil.

Serve with celery sticks, carrot sticks and assorted crudité.

NUTRITIONAL INFORMATION Calories 67, Calories from Fat 50%, Fat 3 g, Saturated Fat 2 g, Cholesterol 18 mg, Sodium 256 mg, Carbohydrates 1 g, Dietary Fiber 0 g, Total Sugars 1 g, Protein 6 g
DIETARY EXCHANGES 1 1/2 lean meat

GUMBO DIP

This dude food dip has all the components of gumbo in a creamy, cheesy dip;
everyone voted "most popular" at a party. Serve with toasted baguette slices or chips.

MAKES: 32 (2-tablespoon) servings · **PREP TIME:** 15 minutes · **COOK TIME:** 15 minutes ·

1 green bell pepper, cored and
   chopped

1 cup sliced okra (frozen is fine)

1/2 cup chopped celery

1 bunch green onions, chopped

1 tablespoon minced garlic

Cajun seasoning to taste

1 pound peeled cooked shrimp,
   coarsely chopped

1 (8-ounce) package reduced-fat
   cream cheese

1/4 cup skim milk

1/2 cup grated Parmesan cheese

1 In large nonstick pan coated with nonstick cooking spray, cook green pepper, okra, and celery about 7 minutes or until almost tender. Add green onions, garlic, and Cajun seasoning; cook a few minutes.

2 Add shrimp, cream cheese, milk, and Parmesan. Stir over low heat until cream cheese is melted and mixture is creamy and bubbly.

*Serve at a party or turn
into a light meal and serve
over rice or pasta to give
you energy.*

*Any seafood may be
substituted for the shrimp.*

NUTRITIONAL INFORMATION Calories 32, Calories from Fat 43%, Fat 2 g, Saturated Fat 1 g, Cholesterol 33 mg, Sodium 69 mg, Carbohydrates 1 g, Dietary Fiber 0 g, Total Sugars 1 g, Protein 5 g
DIETARY EXCHANGES 1 lean meat

BEST BEEF CHILI

It will look like you have super powers when you whip up this hearty and high protein quick favorite chili recipe of ground sirloin, salsa, corn and beef broth to solve your dinner decision.

MAKES: 8 (1-cup) servings · **PREP TIME:** 15 minutes · **COOK TIME:** 20 minutes ·

---

2 pounds ground sirloin

1 teaspoon minced garlic

1 tablespoon chili powder

1 teaspoon ground cumin

1 (16-ounce) jar salsa

2 cups frozen corn

2 (14 1/2-ounce) cans reduced-sodium seasoned beef broth

1 (15-ounce) can black or pinto beans, rinsed and drained

1 In large nonstick pot, brown meat and garlic until done, about 5–7 minutes. Add remaining ingredients.

2 Bring to boil, reduce heat, cook 15 minutes.

Don't be afraid of leftovers! Be sure to make plenty as chili freezes well.

Beef is rich in B6 and B12 vitamins which help blood formation helping boost energy and body functions.

NUTRITIONAL INFORMATION Calories 264, Calories from Fat 21%, Fat 6 g, Saturated Fat 2 g, Cholesterol 62 mg, Sodium 464 mg, Carbohydrates 25 g, Dietary Fiber 5 g, Total Sugars 4 g, Protein 30 g

DIETARY EXCHANGES 1 1/2 starch, 1 vegetable, 3 lean meat

CHICKEN PARMESAN SLIDERS

Chow down on these simple 5-minute sliders with a classic chicken parmesan taste to get rid of that sluggish feeling. Makes a great game day munch, party pick-up, lunch or snack.

MAKES: 12 sliders · **PREP TIME:** 5 minutes · **COOK TIME:** 1 1/2 minutes ·

1 3/4 cups shredded cooked chicken breast (rotisserie), skin removed

1 (8-ounces) tomato sauce

1 teaspoon minced garlic

1 teaspoon basil leaves

1 teaspoon oregano leaves

1 (12-pack) miniature rolls, split in half

3/4 cup shredded part-skim mozzarella cheese

1 Preheat oven to broil. Line baking pan with foil.

2 In bowl, combine chicken, tomato sauce, garlic, basil and oregano.

3 Divide chicken mixture on one half of roll and then sprinkle with cheese. Lay other half of roll on baking pan.

4 Broil both halves 1 1/2–2 minutes or until cheese melted and bread toasted. Watch closely. Put slider back together.

TERRIFIC

Pick up burger buns and turn into sandwiches instead of sliders. Sliders freeze well.

NUTRITIONAL INFORMATION Calories 149, Calories from Fat 25%, Fat 4 g, Saturated Fat 2 g, Cholesterol 23 mg, Sodium 369 mg, Carbohydrates 17 g, Dietary Fiber 1 g, Total Sugars 2 g, Protein 11 g

DIETARY EXCHANGES 1 starch, 1 lean meat

FATIGUE

CHICKEN AND BLACK BEAN ENCHILADA CASSEROLE

Top rated and too good to be true—layers of southwestern seasoned chicken, black beans, enchilada sauce and tortillas, topped with melted cheese creates a scrumptious make-ahead dish.

MAKES: 8 servings · **PREP TIME:** 15 minutes · **COOK TIME:** 35 minutes ·

2 cups shredded cooked chicken breast (rotisserie)

1 teaspoon chili powder

1/2 teaspoon ground cumin

2 tablespoons chopped fresh cilantro

1 (15-ounce) can black beans, rinsed and drained

1 (4.5 ounce) can diced green chiles

1 (10-ounce) can red enchilada sauce

8 (6-inch) corn tortillas, quartered

2 cups shredded reduced-fat Mexican-blend cheese, divided

2/3 cup nonfat plain Greek yogurt

1 Preheat oven 350°F. Coat 11×7×2-inch baking dish with nonstick cooking spray.

2 In bowl, combine chicken, chili powder, cumin, cilantro, black beans and green chiles

3 Spread half of enchilada sauce over bottom of baking dish. Place four quartered tortillas over the sauce, overlapping. Spoon half the chicken mixture over tortillas, and sprinkle with 1 cup cheese and dollop yogurt on top. Next, spoon remaining enchilada sauce, another layer of tortillas, and remaining chicken mixture.

4 Cover dish with foil. Bake 25–30 minutes. Remove foil and sprinkle with remaining 1 cup cheese. Return to oven 5 minutes. Let stand 10 minutes before serving.

SERVING SUGGESTION

Serve with sliced avocados, and sprinkle with cilantro before serving. If you don't like cilantro, leave it out.

NUTRITIONAL INFORMATION Calories 235, Calories from Fat 30%, Fat 8 g, Saturated Fat 4 g, Cholesterol 50 mg, Sodium 740 mg, Carbohydrates 18 g, Dietary Fiber 4 g, Total Sugars 2 g, Protein 23 g

DIETARY EXCHANGES 1 starch, 3 lean meat

CRAB AND SPINACH PASTA

Guys—go gourmet with this easy, exceptionally delicious light, creamy crabmeat and spinach pasta dish.

MAKES: 8 (1-cup) servings · **PREP TIME:** 10 minutes · **COOK TIME:** 20 minutes ·

8 ounces angel hair pasta

1 tablespoon butter

1 tablespoon olive oil

1/2 pound sliced mushrooms

1/2 cup chopped green onions

1/3 cup chopped fresh parsley

1 teaspoon minced garlic

1 tablespoon cornstarch

1 (12-ounce) can fat-free evaporated skim milk, divided

1 /3 cup white wine (or broth)

4 cups packed fresh baby spinach leaves

1 pound back fin lump or white crabmeat, picked of shells

1/3 cup grated Parmesan cheese, optional

1 Cook pasta according to package directions. Drain and set aside.

2 In large nonstick skillet, heat butter and oil and sauté mushrooms, green onions, parsley, and garlic over medium heat about 5 minutes, or until tender.

3 In bowl, combine cornstarch with about 1/2 cup evaporated milk, and mix until smooth. Add to pan and stir continuously.

4 Gradually add wine and remaining milk, stirring until mixture thickens. Reduce heat and add spinach and crabmeat, stirring until spinach wilted.

5 Toss with pasta and sprinkle with Parmesan cheese, if desired.

12 cups uncooked spinach equals 2 cups cooked— that's 12 cups of nutrients packed into 2!

NUTRITIONAL INFORMATION Calories 250, Calories from Fat 17%, Fat 5 g, Saturated Fat 1 g, Cholesterol 49 mg, Sodium 296 mg, Carbohydrates 30 g, Dietary Fiber 2 g, Total Sugars 7 g, Protein 21 g
DIETARY EXCHANGES 1 1/2 starch, 1/2 fat-free milk, 2 lean meat

MEAT SAUCE BOLOGNESE

Restaurant quality with homecooking ease. The term "Bolognese" means a thick, full-bodied meat sauce with vegetables enhanced with wine or milk—I have used both to create my husband's favorite meat sauce.

MAKES: 8 (1-cup) servings · PREP TIME: 15 minutes · COOK TIME: 45 minutes ·

2/3 cup chopped carrots

2/3 cup chopped celery

1 onion, chopped

2 tablespoons minced garlic

2 pounds ground sirloin

1 (6-ounce) can tomato paste

1 (14-ounce) can fat-free beef broth

1 cup red wine

1 (14 1/2-ounce) can diced roasted tomatoes in juice

1 teaspoon dried basil leaves

1 teaspoon dried oregano leaves

1 cup skim milk

1 In large nonstick skillet, sauté carrots, celery, onion, and garlic about 5 minutes. Add meat, stirring and cooking until meat is done.

2 Add tomato paste, beef broth, red wine, tomatoes, basil, and oregano. Bring to boil and cook 5 minutes. Add milk and continue cooking over low heat 20–30 minutes.

NUTRITION NUGGET

Beef is rich in a well-absorbed form of iron which helps your body use oxygen efficiently and prevents anemia.

SERVING SUGGESTION

Serve over pasta like angel hair to soak up the rich sauce. Red wine is an ingredient in the sauce but it also pairs exceptionally well with the meal.

TERRIFIC

Keep it gluten-free and use spaghetti squash as noodles.

NUTRITIONAL INFORMATION Calories 217, Calories from Fat 24%, Fat 6 g, Saturated Fat 2 g, Cholesterol 63 mg, Sodium 352 mg, Carbohydrates 11 g, Dietary Fiber 2 g, Total Sugars 7 g, Protein 27 g

DIETARY EXCHANGES 2 vegetable, 3 lean meat

SAUSAGE AND EGGPLANT PASTA

Beer will get your attention in this high energy tantalizing pasta recipe, with chicken, sausage and eggplant as the star ingredients.

MAKES: 6 (1 1/3-cup) servings · **PREP TIME:** 15 minutes · **COOK TIME:** 20 minutes ·

6 ounces chicken sausage,
  thinly sliced

2 tablespoons olive oil

6 cups peeled and diced eggplant

1 cup lite beer

1 teaspoon minced garlic

1 cup frozen peas

1 teaspoon dried oregano leaves

1 (12-ounce) package penne pasta

1/4 cup grated Parmesan cheese

1 In large nonstick skillet coated with nonstick cooking spray, brown sausage 5 minutes.

2 In same pan, heat oil, and add eggplant; cook over medium heat about 5 minutes or until eggplant is soft and sausage is done. Add beer and garlic, bring to boil, lower heat and reduce beer mixture by about one-third. Add peas and oregano.

3 Meanwhile, cook pasta according to package directions; drain and add to eggplant mixture. Sprinkle with Parmesan cheese.

*Look for different varieties
of chicken sausage.*

NUTRITIONAL INFORMATION Calories 356, Calories from Fat 22%, Fat 9 g, Saturated Fat 2 g, Cholesterol 25 mg, Sodium 233 mg, Carbohydrates 52 g, Dietary Fiber 5 g, Total Sugars 5 g, Protein 15 g

DIETARY EXCHANGES 3 starch, 1 vegetable, 1 lean meat, 1/2 fat

LAMB CHOPS WITH MINT SAUCE

No muscle flexing needed in the kitchen with this quick rub-style marinade that gives the lamb superb flavor.
Pairs perfectly with the simple Mint Sauce.

MAKES: 4 servings · **PREP TIME:** 10 minutes + marinade time · **COOK TIME:** 10 minutes ·

---

3 tablespoons fresh chopped mint

1 teaspoon ground cumin

1 teaspoon garlic powder

1/2 teaspoon ground cinnamon

1 1/2 pounds lamb loin chops

MINT SAUCE

1/4 cup boiling water

1/4 cup chopped fresh mint

1 tablespoon sugar

1 tablespoon cider vinegar

1 In large plastic zip-top resealable bag or glass dish, combine mint, cumin, garlic powder, and cinnamon. Add lamb chops and shake to coat well. Refrigerate until ready to cook.

2 *For the Mint Sauce:* In small bowl, pour boiling water over mint and sugar; let sit 15 minutes. Add vinegar. Set aside.

3 Heat large nonstick pan, coated with nonstick cooking spray, to medium-high heat. Place lamb chops in pan and cook until crusty and browned, about 5 minutes on each side. Serve with Mint Sauce.

NUTRITIONAL INFORMATION Calories 179, Calories from Fat 50%, Fat 10 g, Saturated Fat 3 g, Cholesterol 62 mg, Sodium 117 mg, Carbohydrates 2 g, Dietary Fiber 1 g, Total Sugars 0 g, Protein 20 g

DIETARY EXCHANGES 3 lean meat

CHOCOLATE RAISIN PEANUT BUTTER BARS

Perk up your day with this delectable combination that tastes like chocolate covered raisins with peanut butter.

MAKES: 4 dozen bars · **PREP TIME:** 10 minutes · **COOK TIME:** 25 minutes ·

---

1 (18.25-ounce) package yellow
   cake mix

1/2 cup butter

1 egg

1 tablespoon water

2/3 cup raisins

2/3 cup peanuts

1/3 cup creamy peanut butter

1 cup semi-sweet chocolate chips

1 Preheat oven 350°F. Coat 13×9×2-inch baking pan with nonstick cooking spray.

2 In mixing bowl, combine cake mix, butter, egg, and water until well mixed. Transfer batter to prepared pan. Bake 20–25 minutes or until golden brown.

3 In medium pot or in microwave, combine raisins, peanuts, peanut butter, and chocolate chips over low heat stirring until melted. Spread over baked crust. Refrigerate 1 hour before cutting.

Did you know one cup of chocolate chips has 34 mg of caffeine?

NUTRITIONAL INFORMATION Calories 111, Calories from Fat 43%, Fat 6 g, Saturated Fat 3 g, Cholesterol 9 mg, Sodium 106 mg, Carbohydrates 14 g, Dietary Fiber 1 g, Total Sugars 9 g, Protein 2 g
DIETARY EXCHANGES 1 other carbohydrate, 1 fat

FATIGUE

BERRY SMOOTHIE

Just the quick, healthy pick-me-up you need, morning or afternoon to shake that sluggish feeling!

MAKES: 2 (3/4-cup) servings · PREP TIME: 5 minutes · COOK TIME: None ·

1 cup strawberries, fresh or frozen

1/2 cup blueberries

1 tablespoon sugar

1/4 cup skim milk

1/4 cup nonfat vanilla Greek yogurt

1 In food processor or blender, combine all ingredients until well blended. Serve immediately.

NUTRITION NUGGET

For a more filling smoothie add nut butters like almond or peanut butter as an easy way to add healthy fats and protein. Greek yogurt is a high protein, low sugar version of yogurt.

SERVING SUGGESTION

Turn a smoothie into a heartier snack or light dessert, top with granola and diced fresh fruit.

NUTRITIONAL INFORMATION Calories 104, Calories from Fat 0%, Fat 0 g, Saturated Fat 0 g, Cholesterol 1 mg, Sodium 22 mg, Carbohydrates 22 g, Dietary Fiber 2 g, Total Sugars 18 g, Protein 4 g
DIETARY EXCHANGES 1 fruit, 1/2 fat-free milk

HEART DISEASE

HEART DISEASE
I'M AFRAID OF A BROKEN HEART

WHAT ARE THE RISK FACTORS FOR HEART DISEASE?
IS HEART DISEASE PREDICTABLE?
WHAT CAN YOU DO TO PREVENT HAVING A HEART ATTACK?

Heart disease is the number-one cause of death for men in this country, responsible for over 300,000 deaths annually—about 1 out of every 4 male deaths.[1]

The threat of death from heart disease is real, and it is scary; in fact it is the biggest fear of most men who come to my office—second only to the fear of hair loss! The fear of having a heart attack is especially worrisome for men because in many cases heart attacks are sudden and completely unexpected. In fact, half of the men who die suddenly from heart attacks have *no* previous symptoms.[2]

Men usually make an appointment to see me because a friend or family member suddenly died from a heart attack, and they want to be checked out. As with many other things, men fear the unknown—and most men do not know whether they are at risk for a heart attack.

The truth is, it is not difficult to spot the man who is "supposed" to have the heart attack (see story in Preface: Preventative Health Concept). It simply requires a visit to the physician, answering some screening questions, an exam and some bloodwork. Putting all the pieces together paints a picture of your overall risk. Once you know your risk, you can develop a plan with your physician to make adjustments in your life to reduce your risk. Sound familiar? It should. You do this in other areas of your life every day.

Don't be a victim, and stop being afraid. Visit your physician and have a risk assessment done. Most cardiac deaths are preventable.

What are the Risk Factors for Heart Disease?
- Family History of Heart Attack
- Diabetes
- Hypertension (high blood pressure)
- High Cholesterol
- Tobacco Use
- Male Gender
- Sedentary Lifestyle
- Obesity

What You Can Do:
- Know your risk factors for Heart Disease
- Visit with your primary care physician to determine your overall risk
- Develop a plan to reduce or eliminate any modifiable risk factors
- Develop a plan to regularly screen for heart disease

Important Risk Factors to Modify:
- Eliminate all tobacco use
- Adopt a diet low in saturated fats
- Reduce blood pressure
- Weight reduction through diet/exercise

---

[1] Xu, JQ, Murphy, SL., Kochanek, KD, Bastian, BA. Deaths: Final data for 2013. National Vital Statistics Report. 2016:64(2).

[2] Roger VL, Go AS, Lloyd-Jones DM, Benjamin EJ, Berry JD, Borden WB, et al. Heart disease and stroke statistics—2012 update: a report from the American Heart Association. Circulation. 2012;125(1):e2-220.

What To Eat For Heart Disease

If you show your heart some love, your heart will love you back. Now, that you know the risk factors, it's time to make smart food choices to decrease your risk of heart disease. Foods high in saturated fat have been shown to increase that risk and should be kept below 10% of your total dietary intake according to the *2015–2020 Dietary Guidelines for Americans*. Replace with unsaturated fats, while keeping total dietary fats within the age-appropriate range. Saturated fat is found naturally in many foods, mostly foods from animal fat sources like meat and dairy.

What Else Can You Do?

Include more omega-3 fatty acids in your diet as they must come from food, are essential for the body to function and have been shown to help reduce the risk of heart disease and stroke as well as lower cholesterol and inflammation.

Foods high in fiber also have heart protecting benefits by helping to lower cholesterol. Aim for 38 grams of fiber per day, and after the age of 50 the need drops to 30 grams per day.

Strategies to Lower Saturated Fat Intake:

- Choose packaged foods lower in saturated fats by reading food labels.
- Choose lower fat milk (such as skim or low-fat milk rather than 2% or whole milk)
- Replace ice cream with sherbet or frozen yogurt or use low-fat products.
- Choose meat with "loin" or "round" in the name—for example: ground sirloin.
- Eat skinless chicken or turkey breasts.
- Try to include more beans, fish or chicken.
- Prepare foods using oils instead of solid fats high in saturated fat.
- Use oil-based condiments instead of those made with solid fats (such as butter, stick margarine, cream cheese).
- Unsaturated Fat Sources: peanut butter, avocado, raw nuts, fish (salmon, halibut, tuna), olive oil, canola oil

Foods High in Omega-3 Fatty Acids:

- Salmon
- Walnuts
- Sardines
- Flax Seeds
- Soybeans
- Shrimp
- Tuna

Foods High in Fiber:

- Fruits
- Vegetables
- Whole grains
- Nuts Seeds
- Oatmeal
- Brown Rice
- Beans and Lentils

OATMEAL BANANA PANCAKES

Just about the easiest slam-dunk breakfast, next to cereal and loaded with 'good-for-you' delicious ingredients.

MAKES: about 16 pancakes · PREP TIME: 10 minutes · COOK TIME: 10 minutes ·

2 cups old-fashioned oatmeal

2 cups water

1 banana, cut into chunks

2 tablespoons maple syrup or honey

Dash salt

1 teaspoon vanilla extract

1 In blender or food processor, add all ingredients; blend until smooth. Let stand 5 minutes until batter thickens.

2 In nonstick skillet coated with nonstick cooking spray, pour about 1/4–1/3 cup batter into pan and cook 2-3 minutes on each side or until golden brown.

Sometimes I add a little cinnamon. These pancakes freeze great so make plenty to stock your freezer for a quick breakfast.

Oats, an excellent source of soluble fiber, help keep you feeling full longer, as well as stabilizing blood sugar.

NUTRITIONAL INFORMATION Calories 51, Calories from Fat 13%, Fat 1 g, Saturated Fat 0 g, Cholesterol 0 mg, Sodium 9 mg, Carbohydrates 10 g, Dietary Fiber 1 g, Total Sugars 3 g, Protein 1 g

DIETARY EXCHANGES 1/2 starch

KALE CHIPS

Move over bar food and munch on these simple, crisp crunchy chips that melt in your mouth.

MAKES: 8 servings · **PREP TIME:** 5 minutes · **COOK TIME:** 10 minutes ·

---

1 bunch of curly kale, washed, dried, torn into 2-inch pieces

Salt to taste

1 Preheat oven 400°F. Line baking pan with foil and coat with nonstick cooking spray.

2 Spread kale on prepared pan in single layer. Coat kale lightly with nonstick cooking spray. Season to taste.

3 Bake 8–10 minutes or until kale is crispy and edges brown.

Keep kale a part of your regular menu as only 1 cup provides a good source of fiber, 15% of your daily calcium recommended intake, 180% of vitamin A, and 200% of vitamin C!

NUTRITIONAL INFORMATION Calories 28, Calories from Fat 0%, Fat 0 g, Saturated Fat 0 g, Cholesterol 0 mg, Sodium 22 mg, Carbohydrates 5 g, Dietary Fiber 1 g, Total Sugars 0 g, Protein 2 g

DIETARY EXCHANGES 1 vegetable

CHICKEN TORTILLA SOUP

There are lots of tortilla soup recipes but this quick one-pot soup is truly a first round draft choice for a last minute meal. Check out my recipe for easy-to-make homemade tortilla strips that are SO GOOD!

MAKES: 8 (1-cup) servings · PREP TIME: 20 minutes · COOK TIME: 20 minutes ·

1 onion, chopped

1 teaspoon minced garlic

1 red bell pepper, cored and chopped

3 corn tortillas, cut into small pieces

5 cups fat-free chicken broth, divided

1 teaspoon ground cumin

1 teaspoon dried oregano leaves

2 cups shredded cooked chicken breast (rotisserie)

1 cup frozen corn

1 (4-ounce) can green chiles

1 cup red enchilada sauce

Optional: Tortilla Strips (see recipe below)

For a punch of nutrition, toss chopped zucchini and white or black beans into soup.

Corn tortillas in the soup thickens it and adds tons of flavor. Serve soup topped with chopped green onion, cheese, avocado and tortilla strips.

Use kitchen scissors to easily cut tortilla strips.

1 In large nonstick pot coated with nonstick cooking spray, sauté onion, garlic and bell pepper until tender. Add tortillas and about 1 cup chicken broth, stirring until tortillas are soft and blend into soup

2 Add remaining chicken broth and remaining ingredients. Bring to boil, reduce heat, and simmer 15 minutes.

TORTILLA STRIPS

Make tortilla strips while soup is cooking.

6 (8-inch) corn or flour tortillas (corn tortillas for gluten-free option)

1 Preheat oven 350°F. Coat baking pan with nonstick cooking spray.

2 Cut tortillas into thin strips. Spread on prepared pan and bake 15–20 minutes or until lightly browned. Keep strips in zip lock bags.

NUTRITIONAL INFORMATION Calories 118, Calories from Fat 16%, Fat 2 g, Saturated Fat 0 g, Cholesterol 32 mg, Sodium 357 mg, Carbohydrates 12 g, Dietary Fiber 2 g, Total Sugars 3 g, Protein 13 g
DIETARY EXCHANGES 1/2 starch, 1 vegetable, 1 1/2 lean meat

NUTRITIONAL INFORMATION (TORTILLA STRIPS) Calories 90, Calories from Fat 0%, Fat 0 g, Saturated Fat 0 g, Cholesterol 0 mg, Sodium 255 mg, Carbohydrates 18 g, Dietary Fiber 2 g, Total Sugars 0 g, Protein 3 g
DIETARY EXCHANGES 1 starch

CHICKEN TACO SALAD

This southwestern, hearty high-fiber salad bowl really crushes your hunger.

MAKES: 6 (2-cup) servings · **PREP TIME:** 15 minutes · **COOK TIME:** 15–20 minutes

---

1 (5-ounce) package yellow rice

6 cups mixed salad greens

2 cups shredded cooked chicken breast (rotisserie), skin removed

1 (15-ounce) can black beans, rinsed and drained

1 cup grape or cherry tomato halves

1/2 cup chopped red onion

1/2 cup shredded reduced-fat sharp Cheddar cheese

Salsa Vinaigrette (see recipe below)

1 Prepare rice according to package directions. Cool; set aside.

2 In large bowl, combine cooled rice and all ingredients. Toss with Salsa Vinaigrette.

Try substituting quinoa for yellow rice for a higher-protein, lower-carb option.

Think of beans as the nutritional crouton, sprinkle on salads or in casseroles and soups to boost your fiber intake.

SALSA VINAIGRETTE

Use only whatever needed and save extra for another time.

MAKES: 1 1/2 cups

1 cup salsa

2 teaspoons chili powder

1/2 teaspoon ground cumin

1 tablespoon lime juice

2 tablespoons olive oil

1 In small bowl, whisk together all ingredients.

NUTRITIONAL INFORMATION Calories 327, Calories from Fat 29%, Fat 11 g, Saturated Fat 3 g, Cholesterol 57 mg, Sodium 923 mg, Carbohydrates 36 g, Dietary Fiber 6 g, Total Sugars 4 g, Protein 23 g

DIETARY EXCHANGES 2 starch, 1 vegetable, 2 1/2 lean meat

HEART DISEASE

SOUTHWESTERN SHRIMP SALAD BOWL

Southwestern seasoned shrimp, corn, and black beans tossed with greens in
salsa dressing is the most super satisfying salad known to man.

MAKES: 6 servings · PREP TIME: 10 minutes · COOK TIME: 5 minutes ·

2 tablespoons chili powder

1/2 teaspoon garlic powder

1 teaspoon ground cumin

1 tablespoon lime juice

1 1/2 pounds medium peeled shrimp

6 cups coarsely chopped Romaine lettuce or mixed greens

1 cup frozen corn, thawed

1 (15-ounce) can black beans, rinsed and drained

1 cup salsa

1 cup plain nonfat Greek yogurt

1 In plastic zip-top resealable bag or glass dish, combine chili powder, garlic powder, cumin, and lime juice. Add shrimp and toss to coat.

2 In large nonstick skillet coated with nonstick cooking spray, cook shrimp over medium heat until done, about 5 minutes. Remove from heat.

3 In large bowl, combine lettuce, shrimp, corn and black beans. In small bowl combine salsa and yogurt; set aside. Serve salad with salsa dressing.

Rinse and drain canned beans to reduce sodium.

Complex carbs, lean protein and healthy fat—this salad has it all!

Serve with sliced avocados.

NUTRITIONAL INFORMATION Calories 226, Calories from Fat 7%, Fat 2 g, Saturated Fat 0 g, Cholesterol 183 mg, Sodium 590 mg, Carbohydrates 23 g, Dietary Fiber 5 g, Total Sugars 7 g, Protein 30 g
DIETARY EXCHANGES 1 starch, 1 vegetable, 3 1/2 lean meat

BLACK-EYED PEA AND WILD RICE SALAD

Fresh + convenience = homemade for this nutrition-packed savory salad
with a balsamic-Dijon vinaigrette.

MAKES: 6 cups · PREP TIME: 15 minutes · COOK TIME: 20 minutes ·

1 (4.5-ounce) package long grain and wild rice

1 bunch green onions, chopped

1 red bell pepper, cored and chopped

1 green bell pepper, cored and chopped

1/4 cup chopped fresh parsley

1 teaspoon minced garlic

1 (15-ounce) can black-eyed peas, rinsed and drained

VINAIGRETTE

3 tablespoons olive oil

3 tablespoons balsamic vinegar

1 tablespoon Dijon mustard

2 tablespoons chopped jalapeno peppers

1 Cook wild rice according to package directions. Cool.

2 In large bowl, combine wild rice with green onions, bell peppers, parsley, garlic and black-eyed peas.

3 *To make vinaigrette:* In small bowl, whisk together ingredients.

4 Toss vinaigrette with salad, mixing well. Refrigerate until serving.

SERVING SUGGESTION

Serve as a side to your favorite grilled chicken or meat. Also, perfect for the holidays, especially New Year's Day.

NUTRITIONAL INFORMATION Calories 230, Calories from Fat 27%, Fat 7 g, Saturated Fat 1 g, Cholesterol 0 mg, Sodium 384 mg, Carbohydrates 36 g, Dietary Fiber 7 g, Total Sugars 6 g, Protein 7 g

DIETARY EXCHANGES 2 starch, 1 vegetable, 1 fat

CHICKEN LETTUCE WRAPS

P.F. Chang's introduced us all to lettuce wraps and I can't wait for you to try my healthy, quick version.
Think of this as an Asian taco with lettuce as your shell.

MAKES: 8 (1/2-cup) servings · PREP TIME: 10 minutes · COOK TIME: 10 minutes ·

1 pound ground chicken

1 red bell pepper, cored and chopped

1 teaspoon minced garlic

1/2 cup finely chopped onion

1/4 cup hoisin sauce

1 tablespoon peanut butter

2 tablespoons low-sodium soy sauce

1 tablespoon seasoned rice vinegar

1 tablespoon freshly grated ginger

1 (8-ounce) can water chestnuts, drained and diced

1/2 cup chopped green onions

1 head Butter lettuce

1 In large nonstick skillet, cook ground chicken about 3 minutes, making sure to crumble chicken as it cooks. Add red pepper, garlic, and onion, continuing to cook until chicken is done, about 5 minutes longer.

2 Add hoisin sauce, peanut butter, soy sauce, rice vinegar, ginger, water chestnuts and green onions, stirring about 1 minute or until heated.

3 To serve, spoon chicken mixture into the center of lettuce leaf, taco-style.

TERRIFIC **TIP**

Use Boston, Butter, Bibb or even romaine lettuce.

Look for diced water chestnuts in a can.

NUTRITIONAL INFORMATION Calories 117, Calories from Fat 22%, Fat 3 g, Saturated Fat 1 g, Cholesterol 36 mg, Sodium 306 mg, Carbohydrates 9 g, Dietary Fiber 2 g, Total Sugars 5 g, Protein 14 g

DIETARY EXCHANGES 1/2 other carbohydrate, 2 lean meat

BLACKENED CHICKEN WITH AVOCADO CREAM SAUCE

No boring chicken here! Spicy-seasoned chicken with cool avocado sauce makes an unbeatable combination.

MAKES: 4 servings · **PREP TIME:** 10 minutes · **COOK TIME:** 15 minutes ·

1 1/2 teaspoons paprika

1 1/2 teaspoons ground cumin

1/2 teaspoon cayenne pepper

1 teaspoon onion powder

Salt and pepper to taste

1 1/2 pounds boneless, skinless
   chicken breasts (4 breasts)

1/3 cup nonfat plain Greek yogurt

1 avocado, mashed

1 1/2 teaspoons lemon juice

1/2 teaspoon garlic powder

1 In small bowl, mix paprika, cumin, cayenne pepper, onion powder and season to taste. Rub over chicken breasts.

2 In large nonstick pan coated with nonstick cooking spray, cook chicken over medium-high heat, 5–7 minutes on each side or until done.

3 In small bowl, mix yogurt, avocado, lemon juice, and garlic powder until creamy. Serve over chicken.

Adjust cayenne to your spice preference.

NUTRITIONAL INFORMATION Calories 295, Calories from Fat 37%, Fat 12 g, Saturated Fat 2 g, Cholesterol 110 mg, Sodium 210 mg, Carbohydrates 7 g, Dietary Fiber 4 g, Total Sugars 1 g, Protein 39 g

DIETARY EXCHANGES 1/2 carbohydrate, 5 lean meat

HEART DISEASE

HACIENDA CHICKEN

Call it casual cooking with this easy and effortless chicken with a smoky cumin seasoning
in a simple salsa sauce for a super full-flavored nightly protein-packed dinner.

MAKES: 4 servings · **PREP TIME:** 5 minutes · **COOK TIME:** 30 minutes ·

---

1 1/2 pounds boneless, skinless chicken breasts

1 tablespoon ground cumin

1 onion, thinly sliced

1 cup picante sauce or salsa

1/2 cup nonfat plain Greek yogurt

1 tablespoon all-purpose flour

1/2 cup chopped green onions

1 Sprinkle chicken with cumin. In large nonstick skillet coated with nonstick cooking spray, brown chicken on both sides. Top with sliced onions and picante sauce.

2 Cook, covered, over medium-low heat 25-30 minutes or until chicken is tender.

3 In small bowl mix yogurt and flour. Lower heat and gradually add yogurt to pan, heating but do not boil. Sprinkle with green onions.

Serve with yellow rice.

Pick different flavored salsas to switch up the flavor.

NUTRITIONAL INFORMATION Calories 260, Calories from Fat 18%, Fat 5 g, Saturated Fat 1 g, Cholesterol 109 mg, Sodium 460 mg, Carbohydrates 13 g, Dietary Fiber 1 g, Total Sugars 7 g, Protein 39 g
DIETARY EXCHANGES 2 vegetable, 5 lean meat

CHICKEN WITH TOMATO TOPPING AND MOZZARELLA

I'm not horsing around—this delicious chicken recipe is as good as winning the Triple Crown!
Marinated chicken topped with tomatoes, spinach, and mozzarella cheese.

MAKES: 6 servings · **PREP TIME:** 10 minutes + marinade time · **COOK TIME:** 20 minutes ·

1/4 cup lemon juice

1 teaspoon dried oregano leaves

1 teaspoon paprika

6 (4-ounce) boneless, skinless chicken breasts

3/4 cup chopped onion

1/2 teaspoon minced garlic

1 pint assorted cherry tomato halves

1 1/2 cups fresh baby spinach leaves

Salt and pepper to taste

1/3 cup shredded part-skim mozzarella cheese

1 In plastic zip-top resealable bag or glass dish, combine lemon juice, oregano, and paprika. Add chicken. Refrigerate 1 hour or until ready to cook.

2 Preheat broiler. Line baking pan with foil. Place chicken breasts on pan, discard extra marinade. Broil chicken 7–9 minutes on each side or until chicken is tender.

3 Meanwhile, in nonstick skillet coated with nonstick cooking spray, sauté onion and garlic until tender, 5 minutes. Add tomatoes; sauté few minutes longer. Add spinach, cooking only until leaves are wilted. Season to taste.

4 Divide mixture on top of each chicken breast, sprinkle with mozzarella cheese.

In a serving of only 5 cherry tomatoes, they provide 15% of your daily recommended intake of vitamin A and 10% of vitamin C.

Per 3.5 ounce portion of chicken breast, just by removing the skin saves you over 4 grams of fat and 1 gram of saturated fat.

NUTRITIONAL INFORMATION Calories 176, Calories from Fat 22%, Fat 4 g, Saturated Fat 1 g, Cholesterol 77 mg, Sodium 185 mg, Carbohydrates 7 g, Dietary Fiber 2 g, Total Sugars 3 g, Protein 27 g
DIETARY EXCHANGES 1 vegetable, 3 1/2 lean meat

HEART DISEASE

BLACKENED FISH

Blackening gives fish flavor without the fuss and you'll love my sweet and spicy restaurant quality seasoning. Believe it or not, you can make this recipe "Ferrari fast."

MAKES: 4 servings · **PREP TIME:** 10 minutes · **COOK TIME:** 10 minutes ·

---

2 tablespoons paprika

1 teaspoon chili powder

1/2 teaspoon dried thyme leaves

1 teaspoon garlic powder

1 teaspoon pepper

1/2 teaspoon salt

1 1/2 pounds fish fillets

2 tablespoons olive oil

1 In small bowl or plastic zip-top resealable bag, combine all ingredients, except fish and oil. Coat both sides of fish with seasoning mixture.

2 In large nonstick pan, heat oil over medium-high heat. Place fish in hot pan and cook 2–3 minutes on each side until fish is done and flakes with fork.

Fish is done when center is white and opaque—no longer translucent.

Any fresh fish may be used such as grouper, halibut, tilapia, trout or catfish.

NUTRITIONAL INFORMATION Calories 232, Calories from Fat 36%, Fat 9 g, Saturated Fat 1 g, Cholesterol 63 mg, Sodium 395 mg, Carbohydrates 3 g, Dietary Fiber 2 g, Total Sugars 0 g, Protein 34 g

DIETARY EXCHANGES 4 1/2 lean meat

TROUT WITH DIJON SAUCE AND PECANS

Liven up broiled fish with this simple, scrumptious sauce and toasted pecans.

MAKES: 6 servings · PREP TIME: 10 minutes · COOK TIME: 15 minutes ·

6 (4-ounce) trout fillets

Salt and pepper to taste

1/2 cup Italian bread crumbs

1/4 cup nonfat plain Greek yogurt

1 tablespoon Dijon mustard

1 tablespoon lemon juice

3 tablespoons chopped pecans, toasted

1/2 cup chopped green onions

1 Preheat broiler.

2 Season fish to taste and arrange in oblong baking dish coated with nonstick cooking. Top fish evenly with bread crumbs. Cook under broiler 5–7 minutes, or until fish flakes easily when tested with fork.

3 Meanwhile, in small bowl, combine yogurt, mustard, and lemon juice. Spoon 1 tablespoon sauce over fish and sprinkle with pecans and green onions.

TERRIFIC TIP

To test fish for doneness, prod it with a fork at its thickest point. Properly cooked fish is opaque, has milky white juices and just begins to flake easily. Don't overcook or it will be dry.

NUTRITION NUGGET

Trout is a mild fish rich in amino acids—precursors to protein, important building blocks for healing and tissue repair.

NUTRITIONAL INFORMATION Calories 206, Calories from Fat 32%, Fat 7 g, Saturated Fat 1 g, Cholesterol 67 mg, Sodium 246 mg, Carbohydrates 8 g, Dietary Fiber 1 g, Total Sugars 1 g, Protein 26 g

DIETARY EXCHANGES 3 lean meat, 1/2 starch

BAKED SHRIMP SCAMPI

This rich tasting oven-baked Italian seasoned shrimp topped with a crispy topping is actually super easy to make and will delight the senses. Plus, gives you bragging rights!

MAKES: 4 servings · **PREP TIME:** 15 minutes · **COOK TIME:** 20–25 minutes ·

1 pound medium large shrimp, peeled
2 tablespoons olive oil
2 tablespoons white wine
1 teaspoon minced garlic
1 teaspoon dried oregano leaves
Salt and pepper to taste
1 tablespoon butter, melted
1/2 cup chopped green onions
3 tablespoons lemon juice
1 1/2 cups Panko bread crumbs

1 In shallow baking dish combine shrimp, olive oil, wine, garlic, oregano and season to taste. Let sit about 10 minutes

2 Preheat oven 425°F.

3 In bowl, mix together butter, green onions, lemon juice and Panko bread crumbs. Sprinkle evenly over shrimp in marinade. Bake 20–25 minutes (don't overcook) or until shrimp are done.

SERVING SUGGESTION

Great served over angel hair pasta.

TERRIFIC TIP

Italian bread crumbs may be used instead of Panko.

NUTRITIONAL INFORMATION Calories 256, Calories from Fat 39%, Fat 11 g, Saturated Fat 3 g, Cholesterol 151 mg, Sodium 319 mg, Carbohydrates 19 g, Dietary Fiber 1 g, Total Sugars 1 g, Protein 18 g
DIETARY EXCHANGES 1 1/2 starch, 3 lean meat

CRAWFISH BURGERS

Here's the best Cajun burger around—Crawfish Burgers with Horseradish Sauce atop your favorite bun.
Did you know Louisiana crawfish is low in fat and a good source of protein?

MAKES: 8 crawfish cakes · **PREP TIME:** 15 minutes · **COOK TIME:** 10 minutes ·

---

1 cup saltine cracker crumbs

1 tablespoon Dijon mustard

2 tablespoons light mayonnaise

1 teaspoon hot sauce

1 bunch green onions, chopped

1/3 cup chopped parsley

1/3 cup shredded reduced-fat sharp Cheddar cheese

1 pound Louisiana crawfish tails, rinsed and drained

Salt and pepper to taste

1 tablespoon olive oil

Flour

Optional: Horseradish Sauce (see recipe below)

1 In medium bowl, carefully mix together all ingredients except olive oil and flour.

2 Cover, chill 30 minutes, if time permits. Shape into 8 patties.

3 In large nonstick skillet, heat oil, lightly dust cakes with flour, cook over medium heat 3–5 minutes on each side, or until browned. Serve with Horseradish Sauce.

HORSERADISH SAUCE

Easy sauce with a bite.

1/4 cup nonfat plain Greek yogurt

2 tablespoons light mayonnaise

1 tablespoon lemon juice

2 tablespoons prepared horseradish

1 Combine all ingredients, mix well.

To make ahead of time, mold into patties, and refrigerate, covered, until ready to cook.

For cracker crumbs, place crackers in a food processor or blender.

Make small crawfish patties and pop in miniature buns for delicious sliders.

NUTRITIONAL INFORMATION Calories 134, Calories from Fat 35%, Fat 5 g, Saturated Fat 1 g, Cholesterol 79 mg, Sodium 254 mg, Carbohydrates 9 g, Dietary Fiber 1 g, Total Sugars 1 g, Protein 12 g
DIETARY EXCHANGES 1/2 starch, 2 lean meat

NUTRITIONAL INFORMATION (SAUCE) Calories 25, Calories from Fat 44%, Fat 1 g, Saturated Fat 0 g, Cholesterol 3 mg, Sodium 73 mg, Carbohydrates 3 g, Dietary Fiber 0 g, Total Sugars 1 g, Protein 1 g
DIETARY EXCHANGES Free

HEART DISEASE

LEMON QUINOA

Get some variety in your life with quinoa.
A burst of lemon livens up this simple side—goes great with all entrees.

MAKES: 6 (1/2-cup) servings · **PREP TIME:** 5 minutes · **COOK TIME:** 15 minutes ·

1 1/2 cups water
1 cup quinoa
1/4 cup chopped parsley
2 tablespoons lemon juice
1 teaspoon grated lemon zest
1 tablespoon olive oil
Salt to taste

1 In a small pot, bring water to boil and add quinoa. Lower heat and cook, covered, 15 minutes or until done.

2 Fluff with fork and add remaining ingredients.

Quinoa, a great source of protein and fiber, is a convenient and nutritional whole grain, gluten–free substitute for rice.

NUTRITIONAL INFORMATION Calories 126, Calories from Fat 28%, Fat 4 g, Saturated Fat 1 g, Cholesterol 0 mg, Sodium 5 mg, Carbohydrates 19 g, Dietary Fiber 2 g, Total Sugars 2 g, Protein 4 g
DIETARY EXCHANGES 1 1/2 starch, 1/2 fat

ROASTED LEMON BROCCOLI

Bored with broccoli? You'll be surprised how simple ingredients like lemon and garlic turn broccoli into a delectable, delicious vegetable.

MAKES: 8 (1/2-cup) servings · **PREP TIME:** 5 minutes · **COOK TIME:** 18–24 minutes ·

8 cups broccoli florets

6 cloves garlic, thinly sliced

3 tablespoons olive oil

Salt and pepper to taste

1 teaspoon grated lemon zest

3 tablespoons lemon juice

1 Preheat oven 425°F. Line baking pan with foil and coat with nonstick cooking spray

2 Toss broccoli with garlic and olive oil. Spread on prepared pan. Season to taste.

3 Roast 18–24 minutes or until crisp tender and tips browned.

4 Remove from oven and toss with lemon zest and lemon juice.

Look for pre-washed cut broccoli florets for extra ease.

Broccoli is an anti-inflammatory powerhouse, rich in antioxidants, Vitamin C and carotenoids.

NUTRITIONAL INFORMATION Calories 80, Calories from Fat 55%, Fat 5 g, Saturated Fat 1 g, Cholesterol 0 mg, Sodium 31 mg, Carbohydrates 7 g, Dietary Fiber 2 g, Total Sugars 2 g, Protein 3 g

DIETARY EXCHANGES 1 vegetable, 1 fat

HEART DISEASE

ROASTED HONEY DIJON CARROTS

Roast carrots for simple preparation with maximum flavor. Tossed with honey mustard;
knocks carrots out of the park! (Remember to only roast veggies, not your honey.)

MAKES: 6 (2/3-cup) servings · **PREP TIME:** 5 minutes · **COOK TIME:** 20–25 minutes ·

1 (16-ounce) package baby carrots
1 tablespoon olive oil
2 tablespoons honey
1 tablespoon Dijon mustard
1/4 teaspoon ground ginger

1 Preheat oven 400°F. Cover baking pan with foil and coat with nonstick cooking spray.

2 On baking pan, toss carrots with oil. Roast 20–25 minutes or until carrots are tender.

3 In microwavable cup, microwave honey, mustard, and ginger 20 seconds or until mixed. Toss with roasted carrots.

Carrots are so well known for their extremely high antioxidant beta-carotene content they were named after! Carrots are also a good source of soluble fiber.

NUTRITIONAL INFORMATION Calories 73, Calories from Fat 33%, Fat 3 g, Saturated Fat 0 g, Cholesterol 0 mg, Sodium 78 mg, Carbohydrates 12 g, Dietary Fiber 1 g, Total Sugars 10 g, Protein 1 g
DIETARY EXCHANGES 1 vegetable, 1/2 other carbohydrate, 1/2 fat

FOOD FOR THE MOOD

FOOD FOR THE MOOD
I'M (NOT) HAVING TROUBLE IN THE BEDROOM

WHAT ARE THE CAUSES OF ERECTILE DYSFUNCTION?
WHAT CAN I DO TO FIX THIS?
AT WHAT POINT SHOULD I SEEK MEDICAL ADVICE?

Jack is 48 years old and has come to me to discuss problems with his "sex life." He tells me that he loves his wife and that he thinks she's very pretty, but lately he just tends to avoid situations that may result in intimacy. After going through the usual list of questions, I ask him about his erections. He admits to me that he had a "failure" around a month ago, something that has never happened before and he is deathly afraid of it happening again. His wife is starting to ask questions about his lack of interest.

An erection requires three key components: 1) Plumbing (blood supply), 2) Electricity (nerve supply), and 3) An undistracted brain. The inability to achieve or hold an erection to the point of ejaculation is called erectile dysfunction (ED). ED is caused by either a medical condition (organic), or by something we conjure up in our own minds (psychogenic).

Organic ED is caused by medication that men take for blood pressure issues. Organic ED can also caused from conditions like diabetes that cause a reduction of blood flow through important body tissues. Organic ED can also be associated with testosterone deficiency. Finally, lower back disease can lead to Organic ED issues.

The majority of men who see me for ED issues suffer from psychogenic ED. Psychogenic ED is almost always sudden, and is a result of some new major stress in a man's life, like—getting a promotion. Typically, there is a failure during intimacy because of a mental distraction of some sort. Once the failure is noticed, trying harder simply makes things worse! The failure can lead to questions from a spouse about whether he finds her attractive any longer, and this simply magnifies the situation. So when the next chance at intimacy comes along, a man is even more determined to make things work, which invariably leads to another failure. The harder he tries, the worse it gets. I call it the bedroom death spiral!

Organic ED has a medical cause, and should be diagnosed at the doctor's office. The medical cause of ED should be identified and treated, if possible. Often, something as simple as changing a blood pressure medication may remedy the situation. However, some men may require help from medications called PDE5 inhibitors (Viagra, Cialis, Levitra) that help produce an erection.

Psychogenic ED is relatively easy to fix these days with education, reassurance, and the use of PDE5 inhibitors. These medications "take the brain out of the equation." Once a man as a couple of successful encounters, everything seems to work out just fine, and medication may not be needed any longer.

What to Do If You Begin to Experience ED:
- Make sure you are getting plenty of sleep
- Avoid any alcohol before engaging in intimacy
- Take things slow—remember the days of kissing and hugging?

- Give yourself permission to not be perfect. If you experience a failure, shift your attention to your partner and become a "giver" instead of a "taker."
- If you feel like you need help, a short-term course of medication may be in order. Call your doctor.

Foods to Spice Up Your Romance

Just like the bedroom, the kitchen can be fun too! Cooking doesn't need to be perfect as long as you are having a good time. Did you know that certain nutrients in food may help boost arousal? It was rumored that Casanova ate over 50 raw oysters a day to boost his libido, since oysters are high in zinc content. Zinc is a mineral that aids in the production of testosterone. Other food rich in zinc include crab and lobster so load up on this good seafood. Figs are another aphrodisiac food and are considered a symbol of fertility. We have some fantastic fig recipes and fresh figs go great with cheese.

Don't forget about "hot and spicy foods!" Hot and spicy food generates a physiological response likened to when you get excited, so spice things up in your kitchen with recipes using poblano peppers and be generous with cayenne pepper! Capsaicin is the molecular compound that give peppers like cayenne, green and red chili peppers and Tabasco products, their "spice factor."

Foods to Boost Libido:

- Oysters
- Pine nuts
- Figs
- Poblano peppers
- Crab
- Lobster

Foods to Help You De-stress

Since the doc recommends plenty of de-stress and sleep; cherries are naturally high in the sleepy hormone, melatonin. A handful of cherries might be the perfect late night snack. Shrimp and fish such as cod, tuna and halibut have the highest levels of the natural sedative tryptophan—even higher levels than turkey. Magnesium has been found to decrease the stress hormone, cortisol, giving you a calm and sleepy feeling. You might be surprised that some of your favorite foods are rich in magnesium. These foods include spinach, pumpkin seeds, almonds, dark chocolate and avocado.

Foods to Help You Relax:

- Cherries
- Shrimp
- Halibut, cod, or tuna
- Turkey
- Spinach
- Almonds
- Avocado
- Dark chocolate

MARINATED CRAB FINGERS

Did you know that crab can crank up the libido?
Marinated crab fingers, my personal favorite, are simple and insanely good—a real crowd pleaser.

MAKES: 8 servings · **PREP TIME:** 5 minutes + 1 hour to marinate · **COOK TIME:** None

2 tablespoons lemon juice

1 teaspoon Dijon mustard

1/4 cup balsamic vinegar

2 tablespoons cider vinegar

2 tablespoons olive oil

1 (.7-ounce) package Italian dressing mix

1 bunch green onions, chopped

1 pound crab fingers

1 In bowl, combine all ingredients except crab fingers.

2 Toss crab fingers in mixture and marinate 1 hour, or overnight, in the refrigerator.

TERRIFIC

If you don't have balsamic vinegar, just use red wine vinegar.

Crabs, high in zinc, can trigger a surge in the production of sex hormones.

NUTRITIONAL INFORMATION Calories 118, Calories from Fat 30%, Fat 4 g, Saturated Fat 1 g, Cholesterol 43 mg, Sodium 631 mg, Carbohydrates 6 g, Dietary Fiber 1 g, Total Sugars 4 g, Protein 13 g

DIETARY EXCHANGES 1/2 carbohydrate, 2 lean meat

GUACAMOLE GOES GREEK

Liven up guacamole with Greek flavors for an incredible avocado dip.
RELAX! Let this recipe do all the work.

MAKES: 5 (1/4 cup) servings · **PREP TIME:** 5 minutes · **COOK TIME:** None · ✓

---

1 cup chopped avocado
(1–2 avocados)

1/4 cup finely chopped red onion

1 teaspoon minced garlic

2 tablespoons finely chopped parsley

1/2 teaspoon dried oregano leaves

1 teaspoon olive oil

1 tablespoon lemon juice

1/4 cup crumbled reduced-fat
feta cheese

1 In bowl, gently stir together avocado, onion, and garlic. Add parsley and oregano.

2 Gently stir in olive oil, lemon juice and feta. Refrigerate until serving.

SERVING SUGGESTION

Serve with vegetables like bell pepper squares, cucumbers or squash. Also makes a good spread.

NUTRITION NUGGET

Avocados are rich in magnesium, a mineral which helps you calm down and de-stress. Also, avocados are a good source of heart healthy monounsaturaed fats that help your heart and circulation— good for a healthy sex life.

NUTRITIONAL INFORMATION Calories 117, Calories from Fat 73%, Fat 10 g, Saturated Fat 2 g, Cholesterol 1 mg, Sodium 55 mg, Carbohydrates 7 g, Dietary Fiber 4 g, Total Sugars 1 g, Protein 2 g
DIETARY EXCHANGES 1 vegetable, 2 fat

KALE SALAD WITH DRIED CHERRIES

Kale is rich in vitamins A, C and K but if you do not like kale—forget iceberg and substitute a dark leafy green like spinach for a powerhouse nutrient rich salad. A real "must" for a good night's sleep.

MAKES: 4 (1 1/2-cups servings) · **PREP TIME:** 10 minutes · **COOK TIME:** None ·

---

6 cups baby kale

3 tablespoons dried cherries

1/4 cup sliced red onion

2 tablespoon sunflower seeds

2 tablespoons red wine vinegar

1 tablespoon olive oil

1 teaspoon Dijon mustard

1 teaspoon honey

1 In large bowl, combine kale, cherries, red onion and sunflower seeds.

2 In small bowl, whisk together vinegar, oil, mustard and honey.

3 Toss salad with vinaigrette before serving.

NUTRITION NUGGET *Did you know antioxidant rich cherries may help increase your melatonin levels and improve your sleep?*

NUTRITIONAL INFORMATION Calories 136, Calories from Fat 40%, Fat 7 g, Saturated Fat 1 g, Cholesterol 0 mg, Sodium 65 mg, Carbohydrates 17 g, Dietary Fiber 3 g, Total Sugars 5 g, Protein 6 g
DIETARY EXCHANGES 2 vegetable, 1/2 fruit, 1 1/2 fat

BEER BREAD

What man can refuse beer and bread? A must make four-ingredient, irresistable, and super-simple homemade bread. Perfect addition to any meal.

MAKES: 16 servings · **PREP TIME:** 5 minutes · **COOK TIME:** 50 minutes ·

---

4 cups self-rising flour

1/4 cup sugar

1 (16-ounce) bottle lite beer

2 tablespoons butter, melted

SERVING SUGGESTION

Pairs perfectly with just about anything. I suggest serving it with this menu: Salmon Marsala (page 97), Roasted Southwestern Vegetables, (page 79) and White Chocolate Bundt Cake (page 60).

1 Preheat oven 400°F. Coat 9×5×3-inch loaf pan with nonstick cooking spray.

2 In large bowl, mix together flour, sugar, and beer, mixing only until moistened.

3 Transfer batter into prepared pan. Bake 50 minutes or until golden brown. Remove from oven, pour melted butter over top.

NUTRITIONAL INFORMATION Calories 134, Calories from fat 9%, Fat 1 g, Saturated Fat 1 g, Cholesterol 4 mg, Sodium 411 mg, Carbohydrate 27 g, Dietary Fiber 1 g, Sugars 3 g, Protein 3 g
DIETARY EXCHANGES 2 starch

POBLANO PEPPERS WITH CRABMEAT STUFFING

Excite not only your taste buds—poblano peppers have a mild, slightly sweet heat helping
add to that excited physiological response. Add pop to your peppers with this simple crab stuffing!
Crab, high in zinc, also contributes to stimulation.

MAKES: 8 (1/2-cup stuffing) pepper halves · **PREP TIME:** 10 minutes · **COOK TIME:** 10 minutes ·

1/2 cup light sour cream

1/4 cup Italian bread crumbs

1/2 cup chopped green onions

1/2 cup chopped red bell pepper

1 pound white crabmeat, picked
for shells

1/2 cup shredded reduced-fat
sharp Cheddar cheese

Salt and pepper to taste

4 medium-large poblano peppers,
halved and seeded

1 Preheat oven to 375°F. Coat baking pan with nonstick cooking spray.

2 In bowl, combine all ingredients except halved peppers.

3 Spoon crab mixture into halved peppers and place on prepared pan. Cover with foil and bake 30–35 minutes or until peppers are tender.

4 Remove foil and continue baking 7–10 minutes or until tops are lightly browned.

*Fresh poblanos measure about
4–5 inches long and about
2 1/2 inches wide. Select rich
green peppers without bruises,
wrinkles, or soft spots.*

*These peppers provide
great health benefits in the
capsaicin that give them
their punch and could also
fire up your libido.*

NUTRITIONAL INFORMATION Calories 133, Calories from Fat 24%, Fat 3 g, Saturated Fat 2 g, Cholesterol 52 mg, Sodium 333 mg, Carbohydrates 8 g, Dietary Fiber 1 g, Total Sugars 3 g, Protein 17 g
DIETARY EXCHANGES 1 vegetable, 1/2 starch, 2 lean meat

FIG, PROSCIUTTO AND ARUGULA PIZZA

Sweet and savory and oh-so-alluring, this pizza is even a man pleaser.
Did you know figs are considered a symbol of fertility and revered as an aphrodisiac?

MAKES: 8 servings · **PREP TIME:** 5 minutes · **COOK TIME:** 15 minutes

1 tablespoon olive oil

2 tablespoons fig preserves

1 (12-ounce) thin pizza crust

1 1/2 cups shredded part-skim
   mozzarella cheese

2/3 cup sliced fresh figs

2 ounces prosciutto, cut into pieces

1 cup arugula

1 Preheat oven 425°F.

2 In small dish, combine oil and preserves and spread on crust. Sprinkle with cheese and arrange figs on top.

3 Bake 10–15 minutes or until cheese is melted and crust crisp. Immediately top with prosciutto and arugula.

TERRIFIC TIP

*Serve leftover fig preserves
on a cheese tray with
crackers. Fig preserves and
cheese partner well.*

**NUTRITION
NUGGET**

*Fresh peppery greens pump
up this pizza with nutritious
vitamins A and K.*

*Figs pack calcium, iron,
potassium, zinc and high fiber
making you feel satisfied.*

NUTRITIONAL INFORMATION Calories 281, Calories from Fat 34%, Fat 10 g, Saturated Fat 4 g, Cholesterol 20 mg, Sodium 362 mg, Carbohydrates 36 g, Dietary Fiber 4 g, Total Sugars 10 g, Protein 8 g
DIETARY EXCHANGES 1 1/2 starch, 1 fruit, 1 lean meat, 1 fat

SPICY GLAZED CHICKEN

Spice in your meal can bring heat into the bedroom, especially when protein-rich chicken is infused with this spicy seasoning and honey glaze. Can you take the heat?

MAKES: 4 (4-ounce) servings · **PREP TIME:** 10 minutes · **COOK TIME:** 15 minutes ·

---

1 teaspoon chili powder

2 teaspoons paprika

2 teaspoons garlic powder

1/2 teaspoon red pepper flakes

Salt and pepper to taste

1 pound boneless, skinless chicken breasts

1/3 cup honey

1 tablespoon apple cider vinegar

1 Preheat broiler. Cover baking pan with foil and coat with nonstick cooking spray.

2 In small bowl, mix together chili powder, paprika, garlic powder, red pepper flakes and season to taste. Coat chicken with rub mixture and transfer to prepared pan. Broil 5–7 minutes on each side (or grill) or until chicken is done.

3 In small bowl, mix honey and vinegar. Turn chicken again and baste or coat with honey mixture, cooking a few minutes or until honey starts to thicken and forms a glaze (may smoke a little).

Honey contains large amounts of boron which enhances testosterone levels. Boron also improves metabolism which helps keep you fit.

Don't buy extra vinegar, whatever vinegar you have will work.

NUTRITIONAL INFORMATION Calories 228, Calories from Fat 13%, Fat 3 g, Saturated Fat 1 g, Cholesterol 73 mg, Sodium 146 mg, Carbohydrates 26 g, Dietary Fiber 1 g, Total Sugars 24 g, Protein 25 g

DIETARY EXCHANGES 1 1/2 other carbohydrate, 3 lean meat

CHICKEN PESTO PASTA

Tempt your taste buds with this alluring one-dish–meal recipe guaranteed to score high on your list.
Forget the long ingredient list because it's mainly for the pesto.

MAKES: 10 (1-cup) servings · **PREP TIME:** 15 minutes · **COOK TIME:** 15–20 minutes ·

1 1/2 pounds boneless, skinless chicken breasts, cut into strips
1 onion, chopped
1 (16-ounce) package penne pasta
1/2 cup packed fresh parsley leaves
1/2 cup packed fresh basil leaves
3 cloves garlic
1 tablespoon pine nuts
3 tablespoons olive oil
2 tablespoons water
1 cup fat-free chicken broth
1/2 cup sun-dried tomatoes
1/3 cup sliced black kalamata olives
1/3 cup grated Parmesan cheese

1 In a large nonstick pan, sauté chicken about 5 minutes until browned; add onion and continue cooking until chicken is done.

2 Meanwhile, cook pasta according to package directions, drain and set aside.

3 In food processor, process parsley, basil, garlic and pine nuts until combined. With processor still running, add olive oil in a thin stream and continue processing until smooth and creamy. Add water gradually.

4 Add pesto mixture and broth to chicken, cooking and stirring until well heated. Add pasta, sun-dried tomatoes, olives and cheese.

Take a short cut with a jar of basil pesto found in the grocery.

Pine nuts have long been thought to boost libido due to being rich in the mineral zinc, which helps increase testosterone.

Basil increases circulation with an alluring aroma.

NUTRITIONAL INFORMATION Calories 331, Calories from Fat 26%, Fat 9 g, Saturated Fat 2 g, Cholesterol 46 mg, Sodium 258 mg, Carbohydrates 38 g, Dietary Fiber 2 g, Total Sugars 3 g, Protein 23 g
DIETARY EXCHANGES 2 1/2 starch, 2 lean meat

QUICK TURKEY LASAGNA

People will think you have superpowers when you make this scrumptious SO SIMPLE lasagna with no-boil noodles, jars of marinara sauce, turkey and cheese.

MAKES: 10 servings · PREP TIME: 10 minutes · COOK TIME: 1 hour ·

2 (25-ounce) jars marinara sauce

1 (8-ounce) package no-boil lasagna noodles, divided

1 (15-ounce) container part-skim low-fat ricotta cheese, optional

2 1/4 cups shredded part-skim mozzarella cheese, divided

2 (10-ounce) packages chopped spinach, thawed and drained

3 cups chopped cooked skinless turkey breasts

1 Preheat oven 375°F. Coat 13×9×2-inch pan with nonstick cooking spray.

2 Spread about 1 cup marinara sauce on bottom of pan. Top with one-third noodles, ricotta cheese, if using, 1 cup mozzarella, half the spinach, half the turkey and 1 cup sauce. Repeat layering with one-third noodles, remaining turkey, remaining spinach and 1 cup mozzarella. Top with remaining noodles and sauce.

3 Bake, covered with foil, 1 hour. Uncover and top with remaining 1/4 cup cheese and continue cooking 5 minutes or until cheese is melted.

NUTRITION NUGGET

Turkey contains the amino acid tryptophan, which forms the basis of brain chemicals that make people tired—no wonder you're tired after the Thanksgiving meal.

TERRIFIC TIP

Shredded rotissiere chicken may be used instead of turkey.

NUTRITIONAL INFORMATION Calories 316, Calories from Fat 20%, Fat 7 g, Saturated Fat 3 g, Cholesterol 52 mg, Sodium 790 mg, Carbohydrates 37 g, Dietary Fiber 6 g, Total Sugars 12 g, Protein 26 g
DIETARY EXCHANGES 2 starch, 2 vegetable, 2 1/2 lean meat

HALIBUT WITH TOMATOES IN LEMON GARLIC SAUCE

Light and quick pan seared halibut turns into a guy's gourmet masterpiece with a few fresh ingredients. Halibut is a delicious fish with a delicate flavor.

MAKES: 4 servings · **PREP TIME:** 10 minutes · **COOK TIME:** 15 minutes ·

4 (6-ounce) halibut or cod fish fillets

Salt and pepper to taste

2 tablespoons olive oil, divided

1 pint assorted cherry tomatoes, halved

1 tablespoon minced garlic

1/3 cup white wine

1 lemon

3 tablespoons fresh basil leaves, thinly sliced

1 Let fish come to room temperature and pat dry with paper towel. Season to taste.

2 In large nonstick pan coated with nonstick cooking spray, heat 1 tablespoon oil. Add fish to pan and sear about 2 minutes on each side, depending on thickness. Transfer to plate.

3 Add remaining 1 tablespoon oil to same pan. Heat oil and add tomatoes, garlic and wine. Cook, over low to medium heat, until tomatoes start to burst, about 3–5 minutes.

4 Return fish to pan and squeeze lemon juice on top and sprinkle with fresh basil.

Use shrimp, scallops or your favorite fish with this scrumptious sauce.

Fish is rich in tryptophan, a natural sedative, with halibut and cod, having the highest levels, even more than turkey. Cod is a similar fish to halibut.

NUTRITIONAL INFORMATION Calories 249, Calories from Fat 34%, Fat 9 g, Saturated Fat 1 g, Cholesterol 83 mg, Sodium 7 mg, Carbohydrates 7 g, Dietary Fiber 1 g, Total Sugars 3 g, Protein 33 g

DIETARY EXCHANGES 1 vegetable, 4 1/2 lean meat

SHRIMP IN SPICY TOMATO SAUCE

Heat up your kitchen and your mood with this spicy, simple delicious shrimp in a mild tomato sauce.

MAKES: 4 heaping (1-cup) servings · **PREP TIME:** 10 minutes · **COOK TIME:** 15–20 minutes ·

1 pound large peeled shrimp

Salt and pepper to taste

1 tablespoon olive oil

1/2 cup chopped onion

2 teaspoons minced garlic

1 (15-ounce) can crushed tomatoes

1–1 1/2 teaspoons crushed red pepper flakes (depending on taste)

1 teaspoon dried basil leaves

1 teaspoon dried oregano leaves

1/2 cup fat-free chicken broth

1/2 cup nonfat plain Greek yogurt, room temperature

1 Heat large nonstick skillet coated with nonstick cooking spray. Season shrimp and add to skillet. Cook shrimp about 2–3 minutes per side or until done. Remove from skillet onto plate.

2 In same skillet, heat oil and sauté onion about 3 minutes or until tender. Add garlic and cook another minute. Add tomatoes, red pepper flakes, basil, oregano, and broth.

3 Bring to boil, lower heat and continue cooking about 5 minutes. Remove from heat.

4 Stir in Greek yogurt until smooth and add shrimp.

SERVING SUGGESTION

Serve over your favorite grain or pasta.

TERRIFIC TIP

Make sure to add Greek yogurt off the heat to ensure that it doesn't curdle in the sauce.

NUTRITION NUGGET

Capsaicin gives spicy food the heat and also triggers endorphins which can help satisfy you.

NUTRITIONAL INFORMATION Calories 192, Calories from Fat 20%, Fat 4 g, Saturated Fat 1 g, Cholesterol 184 mg, Sodium 429 mg, Carbohydrates 11 g, Dietary Fiber 2 g, Total Sugars 5 g, Protein 28 g

DIETARY EXCHANGES 2 vegetable, 3 lean meat

BARBECUE SHRIMP NEW ORLEANS STYLE

Pretend you're on a trip to New Orleans with my easy, better-for-you popular BBQ shrimp recipe.
This shrimp dish is screaming for a good Chardonnay for the recipe and for you!

MAKES: 4–6 servings · **PREP TIME:** 5 minutes · **COOK TIME:** 15 minutes ·

1/4 cup olive oil

1/4 cup fat-free creamy Italian dressing

1 tablespoon minced garlic

1 teaspoon onion powder

1/4 teaspoon cayenne pepper

1/4 cup Worcestershire sauce

1 tablespoon paprika

2 teaspoons dried oregano leaves

2 teaspoons dried thyme leaves

Salt and pepper to taste

2 pounds large shrimp, unpeeled

1/3 cup white wine

1/2 cup fat-free chicken broth

1 In large nonstick skillet, combine oil, Italian dressing, garlic, onion powder, cayenne pepper, Worcestershire sauce, paprika, oregano, thyme, salt and pepper over medium heat until sauce begins to boil.

2 Add shrimp, cook 5 minutes. Add wine and broth, cook another 5–7 minutes or until shrimp are done.

TERRIFIC

Peeled shrimp may be used in the recipe if desired, but peeling the shrimp is actually a lot of fun, just have plenty of paper towels.

SERVING

Serve with French bread (you must dip it into the delicious sauce) and Angel Hair Pasta (page 131).

NUTRITIONAL INFORMATION Calories 221, Calories from Fat 40%, Fat 10 g, Saturated Fat 1 g, Cholesterol 212 mg, Sodium 474 mg, Carbohydrates 6 g, Dietary Fiber 1 g, Total Sugars 2 g, Protein 27 g

DIETARY EXCHANGES 1/2 other carbohydrate

WASABI CRAB CAKES WITH GINGER SAUCE

Amp it up a notch in the kitchen and in the bedroom with fiery wasabi and soy sauce seasoned crab cakes perfectly paired with the delectable Ginger Sauce. Fresh ginger is a must for this remarkable sauce.

MAKES: 8 servings · **PREP TIME:** 15 minutes + refrigeration time · **COOK TIME:** 10 minutes ·

1/2 cup chopped green onions

3 tablespoons light mayonnaise

1 egg

1 1/2 tablespoons wasabi paste (according to taste)

2 teaspoons seasoned rice vinegar

2 teaspoons low-sodium soy sauce

1 teaspoon lemon juice

1 1/2 cups panko bread crumbs, divided

1 pound white or lump crabmeat, picked through for shells

GINGER SAUCE

3 tablespoons light mayonnaise

3 tablespoons nonfat Greek plain yogurt or sour cream

2 tablespoons grated fresh ginger

1 teaspoon seasoned rice vinegar

1 In bowl, combine green onions, mayonnaise, egg, wasabi, rice vinegar, soy sauce, and lemon juice. Fold in 1/2 cup panko crumbs and crabmeat.

2 Form crab mixture into 8 patties, pat remaining 1 cup panko crumbs onto both sides of patties. For best results, refrigerate at least 1 hour before cooking.

3 *For the Ginger Sauce:* In small bowl, combine all ingredients. Set aside.

4 Heat nonstick skillet coated with nonstick cooking spray over medium heat and cook crab cakes 3–5 minutes on each side or until golden brown. Serve with Ginger Sauce.

Make ahead, refrigerate and cook when ready to serve.

Freeze fresh ginger to have on hand.

The ginger scent stimulates circulation.

NUTRITIONAL INFORMATION Calories 154, Calories from Fat 25%, Fat 4 g, Saturated Fat 0 g, Cholesterol 70 mg, Sodium 463 mg, Carbohydrates 13 g, Dietary Fiber 1 g, Total Sugars 2 g, Protein 15 g

DIETARY EXCHANGES 1 starch, 2 lean meat

TUNA TACOS WITH WASABI CREAM AND MANGO SALSA

Tuna, rich in tryptophan, a natural sedative, makes this causal quick tuna taco perfect for an easy relaxing dinner. Forget the traditional taco condiments because the fiery Wasabi Cream and fresh Mango Salsa is all you need.

MAKES: 4 tuna tacos · **PREP TIME:** 15 minutes · **COOK TIME:** 5 minutes ·

---

1 teaspoon olive oil

10–12 ounces ahi tuna (1-inch thick)

2 teaspoons taco seasoning mix

4 (8-inch) flour or corn tortillas

WASABI CREAM

1/3 cup nonfat Greek plain yogurt

1 teaspoon lime juice

1/8–1/4 teaspoon wasabi, depending on taste

Mango Salsa (see recipe below)

1 Heat oil in pan until hot. Season tuna on both sides with taco seasoning mix and add to hot pan. Sear 1 minute per side or until tuna is cooked on the outside, but rare inside. Set aside.

2 Heat tortillas in microwave, covered with damp paper towel, 30 seconds.

3 *For the Wasabi Cream:* In small bowl, combine all ingredients.

4 Fill tortillas with tuna, top with Wasabi Cream and serve with Mango Salsa.

Wasabi is sold in most grocery stores as paste or in small container where sushi is.

Mangos have aphrodisiac properties, increase virility in men, and are loaded with vitamin E helping to regulate hormones.

MANGO SALSA

MAKES: 1 cup

1/3 cup chopped avocado

1/2 cup chopped mango

2 tablespoons chopped red onion

1 teaspoon chopped jalapeno

1 tablespoon lime juice

1 In small bowl, combine all ingredients.

NUTRITIONAL INFORMATION Calories 273, Calories from Fat 14%, Fat 4 g, Saturated Fat 1 g, Cholesterol 33 mg, Sodium 465 mg, Carbohydrates 31 g, Dietary Fiber 4 g, Total Sugars 4 g, Protein 27 g
DIETARY EXCHANGES 1 1/2 starch, 1 vegetable, 3 lean meat

BAKED ITALIAN OYSTERS

The classic aphrodisiac food, oysters! Cassanova was rumored to have eaten over 50 oysters to boost his libido—worth a shot! This rich oyster dish with Italian flavor has New Orleans roots.

MAKES: 10-12 servings · **PREP TIME:** 15 minutes · **COOK TIME:** 25-30 minutes ·

2 pints oysters, drained
1/3 cup olive oil
1 teaspoon minced garlic
1/3 cup chopped parsley
1 bunch green onions, chopped
2 cups Italian bread crumbs
1/3 cup grated Parmesan cheese
1/4 cup lemon juice

1 Preheat oven to 400°F. Coat shallow oblong 2-quart baking dish with nonstick cooking spray.

2 Place drained oysters on in prepared baking dish.

3 In bowl, combine remaining ingredients, spread evenly over oysters. Bake 25–30 minutes or until oysters are done and topping is browned.

NUGGET

Oysters are high in zinc, which helps increase testosterone. Also high in dopamine hormone which is believed to work for increasing libido.

SERVING
SUGGESTION

Serve oysters with Barbecue Shrimp (page 54) and Angel Hair Pasta (page 131) and you'll feel like you're on a trip to New Orleans.

NUTRITIONAL INFORMATION Calories 193, Calories from Fat 42%, Fat 9 g, Saturated Fat 2 g, Cholesterol 40 mg, Sodium 405 mg, Carbohydrates 19 g, Dietary Fiber 2 g, Total Sugars 2 g, Protein 9 g
DIETARY EXCHANGES 1 1/2 starch, 1 lean meat, 1 fat

PEPPER DIJON BEEF TENDERLOIN

For dinner parties or gatherings, this most amazing meat sets the mood for a "real deal-maker" dinner.
A no fail, winning recipe and definitely on my short list.

MAKES: 20–24 servings · **PREP TIME:** 5 minutes + marinating time · **COOK TIME:** 45 minutes ·

---

1 (5–6 pound) whole tenderloin, trimmed of excess fat

Salt and pepper to taste

1/2 cup fat-free Italian dressing

1/2 cup Worcestershire sauce

1/2 cup Dijon mustard

Coarsely cracked black pepper

1 Lay tenderloin in glass dish and season to taste.

2 Cover and pat tenderloin with Italian dressing and Worcestershire sauce. Cover with plastic wrap and refrigerate 48 hours; time permitting. Let meat come to room temperature before cooking (at least one hour).

3 Preheat oven 500°F. Pour off marinade, cover meat with Dijon mustard and heavily with cracked black pepper. Transfer to baking pan. Cook 500°F for 12 minutes and reduce temperature to 275°F and cook another 25–30 minutes depending on doneness.

SERVING SUGGESTION

Serve with Quick Caesar Salad (page 86), Pesto Potatoes (page 138) and Pull Apart Bread (page 153).

TERRIFIC TIP

Remember to start marinating 48 hours before. Be sure to let meat come to room temperature before cooking.

NUTRITION NUGGET

Red meat is a good source of zinc— so give your libido a boost since zinc raises testosterone.

NUTRITIONAL INFORMATION Calories 148, Calories from Fat 39%, Fat 6 g, Saturated Fat 2 g, Cholesterol 59 mg, Sodium 242 mg, Carbohydrates 1 g, Dietary Fiber 0 g, Total Sugars 0 g, Protein 21 g

DIETARY EXCHANGES 3 lean meat

DOUBLE CHOCOLATE BROWNIES

Dark chocolate gives you an aphrodisiac dose for the perfect chocoholic sweet ending to a fun night.
These super simple moist rich brownies begin with a brownie mix!

MAKES: 48 brownies · **PREP TIME:** 10 minutes · **COOK TIME:** 25 minutes ·

1 (21.5-ounce) package original brownie mix

2 eggs

1/3 cup canola oil

1/4 cup water

1/3 cup dark chocolate chips (1/2 cup for more chocolate)

3 tablespoons butter

2 tablespoons cocoa (dark cocoa preferred)

2 cups confectioners' sugar

2 tablespoons skim milk

1 teaspoon almond extract

1 Preheat oven 350°F. Coat 13×9×2-inch baking pan with nonstick cooking spray.

2 In bowl, combine together brownie mix, eggs, oil, and water until well mixed. Stir in chocolate chips.

3 Transfer to prepared pan. Bake 23–25 minutes (don't overcook). Cool.

4 In mixing bowl, beat butter, cocoa, confectioners' sugar, milk, and almond extract until creamy. Spread on top brownies.

Look for dark cocoa in the stores. Most cookies and brownies freeze well, so make ahead of time, cut into squares and pop out a few when you are craving food for the mood.

NUTRITIONAL INFORMATION Calories 108, Calories from Fat 37%, Fat 4 g, Saturated Fat 1 g, Cholesterol 11 mg, Sodium 45 mg, Carbohydrates 16 g, Dietary Fiber 0 g, Total Sugars 12 g, Protein 1 g
DIETARY EXCHANGES 1 carbohydrate, 1 fat

WHITE CHOCOLATE BUNDT CAKE

These ingredients aren't touted as aphrodisiacs, but you're guaranteed
"a party in your mouth" and an OMG reaction.

MAKES: 16 serving · **PREP TIME:** 10 minutes · **COOK TIME:** 40–45 minutes ·

1 (18 1/4-ounce) box yellow cake mix

1 (4-serving) box instant cheesecake pudding and pie filling mix

1 cup nonfat vanilla or plain Greek yogurt

1/4 cup canola oil

2/3 cup skim milk

1 egg

3 egg whites

1/2 cup white chocolate chips

1/2 cup chopped pecans

1 cup confectioners' sugar

2 tablespoons skim milk

2 teaspoons almond extract

1 Preheat oven 350°F. Coat 10-inch nonstick Bundt pan with nonstick cooking spray.

2 In mixing bowl, combine cake mix, pudding mix, yogurt, oil, milk, egg, and egg whites, mixing until well combined. Stir in white chocolate chips and pecans.

3 Transfer to Bundt pan. Bake 40–45 minutes or until wooden pick inserted comes out clean. Cool cake 10 minutes before inverting on serving plate.

4 Meanwhile, in small bowl, mix confectioners' sugar, milk and almond extract. Drizzle glaze over warm cake.

I love adding fresh blueberries to this cake for an incredible and indulgent simple Blueberry White Chocolate Cake (use 2 cups blueberries) or add chocolate chips and coconut.

Vanilla pudding may be substituted for cheesecake pudding.

NUTRITIONAL INFORMATION Calories 299, Calories from Fat 33%, Fat 11 g, Saturated Fat 3 g, Cholesterol 14 mg, Sodium 336 mg, Carbohydrates 47 g, Dietary Fiber 0 g, Total Sugars 33 g, Protein 5 g

DIETARY EXCHANGES 3 other carbohydrate, 2 fat

OBESITY & DIABETES

OBESITY & DIABETES
WHY CAN'T I LOSE WEIGHT?

WHAT IS DIABETES?
WHY DO PEOPLE WITH DIABETES TEND TO BE OVERWEIGHT?
WHAT CAN I DO TO HELP FIGHT OBESITY?

Daniel comes to me complaining that he can't lose weight. He has been following a diet and exercise regimen for the past several months. Despite his efforts, he has not lost a single pound. He is 38 years old and overweight. His abdomen is large yet his legs and arms are normal looking. His family history is significant in that his father and older brother have "diabetes." Lab work confirms what I already suspect; his fasting blood sugar is elevated, as are his cholesterol and triglycerides. I tell Daniel that like his father and brother, he too has Type II Diabetes.

Obesity, insulin resistance, and diabetes are three bad players in a vicious cycle of problems. Each of these problems feed the other. Insulin Resistance leads to obesity, and obesity ultimately leads to diabetes, which in turn causes more obesity. The root cause of the problem is a "resistance" to insulin that occurs at the cellular level. The physiology is complex, but it boils down to a constant surplus of blood sugar (glucose), which gets stored as fat.

Why does it matter? Diabetes is the leading risk factor for many serious medical conditions, the most dangerous being heart attack and stroke. Diabetes also leads to medical problems such as blindness, chronic kidney failure, and peripheral vascular disease. If diet and exercise are not enough, your doctor may prescribe medications to reduce the amount of excess glucose in your blood.

So why can't Daniel lose weight? While Daniel is doing a good job dieting and exercising, it might not be enough to lead to weight loss. Daniel requires medication to help reduce the glucose in his blood.

After prescribing the appropriate medication, Daniel begins to lose weight rapidly. Within 6 months, he has lost 40 pounds, feels energized and better understands his lifetime commitment.

No Magical Diabetes Diet

With 64% of Americans either overweight or obese and a projected 44 million to have diabetes in the next 20 years we need to make some changes! But the thing is, there is no magical diabetes diet. Everyone should be practicing the same well-balanced healthy lifestyle that is required for diabetics—whole nutritious foods that are moderate sugar, healthy fat and portion control.

"D" Highlights ADA Diabetic Recipes

When you choose unprocessed whole foods, low in simple carbohydrates, you are triggering less insulin while giving your cells nutrients it can use for energy. Fiber, healthy fats, fruits, vegetables and lean protein should be the basis of not just diabetics' diets but everyone's for optimum health. I included a 'D' on recipes throughout the book to highlight these recipes that coincide with the American Diabetes Association recipe guidelines.

A diagnosis of obesity, insulin resistance or diabetes puts you at a greater risk of developing heart disease, arthritis and cancer—in fact, heart disease is the #1 killer of people with diabetes. Because of the crossover of obesity and diabetics health concerns, refer to other trim and terrific recipes and information in this book, especially the Heart Disease Chapter.

SUPER SALSA

Fresh and simple! It's hard to believe all you have to do is open jars of salsa, a can of Mexican-style corn and add avocado for this super salsa recipe.

MAKES: 24 (2-tablespoon) servings · PREP TIME: 5 minutes · COOK TIME: None ·

---

2 cups salsa (or fresh salsa)

1 (11-ounce) can Mexican-style corn, drained

1 avocado, diced

2 tablespoons lemon juice

1 Combine all ingredients in medium bowl.

Did you know:
1/2 cup salsa = 1 serving
of vegetables?

Have fun and use red pepper
squares or cucumber rounds
as low carb chips to dip.

NUTRITIONAL INFORMATION Calories 32, Calories from Fat 37%, Fat 1 g, Saturated Fat 0 g, Cholesterol 0 mg, Sodium 119 mg, Carbohydrates 4 g, Dietary Fiber 1 g, Total Sugars 1 g, Protein 1 g

DIETARY EXCHANGES 1 vegetable

CRISPY ROASTED CHICKPEAS

Looking for a grab-and-go snack? Parmesan cheese and garlic roasted chickpeas make a slam dunk crunchy savory snack. Top salads and soups like croutons. You'll want to double or triple this recipe—they are that good!

MAKES: 4 (1/4-cup) servings · PREP TIME: 5 minutes · COOK TIME: 30–35 minutes ·

1 (15 1/2-ounce) can chickpeas, rinsed and drained
2 teaspoons olive oil
1 tablespoon grated parmesan cheese
1/2 teaspoon garlic powder
Pepper to taste

1 Preheat oven 400°F. Line baking pan with foil and coat with nonstick cooking spray.

2 Remove skins of chickpeas by rubbing chickpeas between fingers. Skin should slide off. Discard chickpea skins. Dry with paper towel.

3 Transfer to bowl and toss with remaining ingredients. Add chickpeas to baking pan in single layer.

4 Bake 30–35 minutes until golden and crispy, shaking pan halfway through.

TERRIFIC  TIP

Call them chickpeas or garbanzo beans, this versatile bean is high in fiber and protein making them a good diabetic snack choice.

NUGGET

Garlic salt elevates the sodium in the recipe, so that's why garlic powder makes a good option.

NUTRITIONAL INFORMATION Calories 179, Calories from Fat 26%, Fat 5 g, Saturated Fat 1 g, Cholesterol 1 mg, Sodium 253 mg, Carbohydrates 26 g, Dietary Fiber 0 g, Total Sugars 0 g, Protein 8 g
DIETARY EXCHANGES 1 1/2 starch, 1/2 lean meat, 1/2 fat

SHRIMP REMOULADE

Show off your culinary skills with this simple remoulade sauce recipe.
Serve on a bed of lettuce for a light lunch or fabulous first course.

MAKES: 6 (1/3-cup) servings · **PREP TIME:** 15 minutes · **COOK TIME:** None ·

---

1 pound medium peeled shrimp, seasoned and cooked

2 tablespoons light mayonnaise

2 tablespoons Creole or grainy mustard

1 tablespoon ketchup

1 tablespoon lemon juice

Dash hot sauce

1/4 cup chopped green onions

2 tablespoons finely chopped red onion

2 tablespoons chopped fresh parsley

1 Place shrimp in bowl.

2 In another small bowl, mix together the remaining ingredients and toss with shrimp. Refrigerate until serving.

Shrimp counts with shells per pound: small 36/45, medium 31/35, large 21/30.

Serve in martini glasses on mixed greens for appetizer, serve as dip or top salad.

You can also use crab or Louisiana crawfish with the remoulade sauce.

NUTRITIONAL INFORMATION Calories 88, Calories from Fat 21%, Fat 2 g, Saturated Fat 0 g, Cholesterol 123 mg, Sodium 235 mg, Carbohydrates 2 g, Dietary Fiber 0 g, Total Sugars 1 g, Protein 15 g

DIETARY EXCHANGES 2 1/2 lean meat

PEAR CHOPPED SALAD

You'll forget you're eating a salad with this combination of crisp pears, tart cherries, bacon and feta over romaine lettuce. Toss with your favorite balsamic vinaigrette or combination of olive oil and balsamic vinegar.

MAKES: 8 (1-cup) servings · **PREP TIME:** 10 minutes · **COOK TIME:** None ·

---

6 cups chopped romaine lettuce

2 medium pears, chopped

1/3 cup dried cherries or cranberries

1/3 chopped pecans, toasted

1/3 cup chopped red onion

6 slices crisp-cooked turkey bacon, crumbled

1/3 cup crumbled reduced-fat feta cheese

Balsamic vinaigrette of choice

1 In large bowl, combine lettuce, pears, cherries, pecans, red onion, bacon and feta.

2 Toss with your favorite vinaigrette before serving.

Apples may be substituted for the pears.

Pears are a good source of fiber—6 grams of fiber per medium size pear—helping to keep your blood sugar balanced.

Vinaigrette is not included in nutritional information.

NUTRITIONAL INFORMATION Calories 127, Calories from Fat 38%, Fat 5 g, Saturated Fat 1 g, Cholesterol 17 mg, Sodium 283 mg, Carbohydrates 14 g, Dietary Fiber 3 g, Total Sugars 8 g, Protein 6 g
DIETARY EXCHANGES 1 fruit, 1 lean meat, 1/2 fat

MEATY PITA NACHOS

This recipe trumps bar food nachos and will tame those hunger pains.
Made with crispy pita chips, meat, fresh Mediterranean condiments and cool cucumber sauce!

MAKES: 8 servings · **PREP TIME:** 15 minutes · **COOK TIME:** 15 minutes ·

6 whole-wheat pitas, split and each half cut into 8 triangles

1/2 pound ground sirloin

1/2 cup chopped onion

1/2 teaspoon minced garlic

1/2 teaspoon ground cumin

Tzatziki Sauce (see recipe below)

1/2 cup chopped red onion

1/2 cup halved grape tomatoes

1/2 cup chopped cucumber

1/3 cup crumbled reduced-fat feta cheese

3 tablespoons sliced Kalamata olives

1. Preheat oven 400°F. Coat baking pan with nonstick cooking spray.

2. Lay pita triangles on baking pan and bake about 10 minutes or until crispy. Remove from oven.

3. In nonstick skillet, cook meat, onion, and garlic until meat is done. Add cumin; set aside.

4. Arrange baked pitas on plate. Spread meat over pitas and top with Tzatziki Sauce. Sprinkle with red onion, tomatoes, cucumber, feta and olives.

SERVING SUGGESTION

Serve as appetizer or main meal.

Buy pita chips (like my sister did) and you don't have to bake pitas.

Greek yogurt is an excellent low fat, low sugar, high protein substitute for plain yogurt or even sour cream.

TZATZIKI SAUCE

A classic Greek and Turkish creamy sauce that also makes a great dip.

1 cup nonfat plain Greek yogurt

1/2 cup peeled and seeded finely diced cucumber

1 teaspoon minced garlic

1 teaspoon white wine vinegar

1 tablespoon lemon juice

Salt and pepper to taste

1. In small bowl, combine all ingredients.

NUTRITIONAL INFORMATION Calories 204, Calories from Fat 17%, Fat 4 g, Saturated Fat 1 g, Cholesterol 17 mg, Sodium 411 mg, Carbohydrates 30 g, Dietary Fiber 4 g, Total Sugars 3 g, Protein 15 g
DIETARY EXCHANGES 2 starch, 1 1/2 lean meat

GREEN CHILE CHICKEN CHILI

Go green and remake your chili with pantry ingredients like cans of chicken broth,
beans and green chiles combined with rotisserie chicken.

MAKES: 5 (1-cup) servings · PREP TIME: 15 minutes · COOK TIME: 15 minutes ·

2 cups fat-free, low-sodium chicken broth, divided

2 (15-ounce) cans Great Northern beans, rinsed and drained, divided

1 cup chopped onion

1 tablespoon minced garlic

2 teaspoons all-purpose flour

2 (4-ounce) cans diced green chiles, drained

1 tablespoon ground cumin

1 1/2 cups shredded cooked chicken breasts (rotisserie), skin removed

1 In blender, place 1/2 cup chicken broth and 1 can beans and blend until smooth.

2 In large nonstick pot coated with nonstick cooking spray, sauté onion until tender, about 5 minutes. Add garlic and flour, stirring 1 minute. Add chiles, cumin, bean mixture and remaining 1 can beans.

3 Bring to boil, reduce heat and cook until slightly thickened, about 5 minutes. Add chicken and cook until heated, about 2 minutes.

 TERRIFIC **TIP**

White beans such as navy beans (smaller) or cannellini beans (larger) may be substituted for Great Northern beans.

 NUTRITION NUGGET

Sometimes just using a low-sodium broth can keep a recipe diabetic-friendly!

 SERVING SUGGESTION

Serve with chopped cilantro, avocado and cheese.

NUTRITIONAL INFORMATION Calories 222, Calories from Fat 8%, Fat 2 g, Saturated Fat 0 g, Cholesterol 36 mg, Sodium 394 mg, Carbohydrates 27 g, Dietary Fiber 7 g, Total Sugars 6 g, Protein 22 g
DIETARY EXCHANGES 1 1/2 starch, 1 vegetable, 2 lean meat

CHICKEN TOSTADAS

Layers of Tex-Mex flavors have your taste buds singing! The ingredient list looks long but these tostadas are easy to make, I promise! Layer guacamole, beans, tomato mixture, chicken and cheese. Delish!

MAKES: 8 tostados · **PREP TIME:** 20 minutes · **COOK TIME:** 10 minutes ·

1 tablespoon ground cumin

1 tablespoon dried chili powder

1 teaspoon garlic powder, divided

1 teaspoon paprika

1 1/4 pounds boneless, skinless chicken breasts, cubed

2 cups cherry tomato halves

1/4 cup finely chopped red onion

1 teaspoon minced garlic, divided

1/4 cup finely chopped cilantro leaves

1 teaspoon olive oil

1 (15-ounce) can black beans, rinsed and drained

1 large avocado

3 tablespoons nonfat plain Greek yogurt

2 tablespoons lime juice

8 tostada shells

1/2 cup shredded reduced-fat Mexican-blend cheese

1 In small bowl, mix together cumin, chili powder, garlic powder, and paprika. Toss chicken with seasonings. In large nonstick pan coated with nonstick cooking spray, cook chicken, stirring, until browned and cooked through; set aside.

2 In another bowl, combine tomatoes, red onion, 1/2 teaspoon garlic, 1/4 cup cilantro and olive oil. Season to taste; set aside. In another bowl, mix beans with remaining 1/2 teaspoon garlic; set aside.

3 In small bowl, mash avocado and add yogurt, lime juice and season to taste, mixing until smooth.

4 *To assemble:* Spread guacamole on tostada and layer beans, tomato mixture, chicken and cheese.

 TERRIFIC **TIP**

Prepare chicken, salsa and avocado mixtures ahead. Refrigerate to make tostadas on your time frame.

NUTRITION NUGGET

A serving of only 5 cherry tomatoes provides 15% of your daily recommended intake of vitamin A and 10% of vitamin C. This is a high fiber recipe making it good for blood sugar control and weight maintenance.

NUTRITIONAL INFORMATION Calories 297, Calories from Fat 37%, Fat 12 g, Saturated Fat 2 g, Cholesterol 50 mg, Sodium 405 mg, Carbohydrates 24 g, Dietary Fiber 7 g, Total Sugars 3 g, Protein 23 g

DIETARY EXCHANGES 1 1/2 starch, 1 vegetable, 3 lean meat, 1/2 fat

CHICKEN FAJITA PIZZA

Fajitas and pizza in one recipe—a deliciously unbeatable combination
and this favorite pizza is even easy and healthy!

MAKES: 8 servings · **PREP TIME:** 10 minutes · **COOK TIME:** 10 minutes ·

2 cups shredded cooked chicken breast (rotisserie), skin removed

1 teaspoon chili powder

1 medium onion, thinly sliced

1 medium green, red or yellow bell pepper, cored and thinly sliced

1 thin pizza crust

2/3 cup picante sauce

1 cup shredded reduced-fat Mexican-blend cheese

1 Preheat oven 425°F. Coat pizza pan with nonstick cooking spray.

2 In bowl, combine chicken with chili powder.

3 In small nonstick skillet coated with nonstick cooking spray, sauté onion and green pepper, cooking until crisp tender.

4 Top pizza crust with picante sauce, chicken, onion mixture and cheese. Bake 8–10 minutes or until crust is lightly brown.

Pick up sliced assorted bell peppers or raid the salad bar to use red, green and yellow peppers.

NUTRITIONAL INFORMATION Calories 210, Calories from Fat 27%, Fat 6 g, Saturated Fat 2 g, Cholesterol 38 mg, Sodium 469 mg, Carbohydrates 19 g, Dietary Fiber 1 g, Total Sugars 3 g, Protein 18 g
DIETARY EXCHANGES 1 starch, 1 vegetable, 2 lean meat

CHICKEN FRICASSEE

Better known as smothered chicken, this slow simmered recipe creates fall-apart tender chicken in the most flavorful gravy served over rice. Comfort food—just like mom made!

MAKES: 6–8 servings · **PREP TIME:** 15 minutes · **COOK TIME:** 1 hour 20 minutes ·

2 tablespoons olive oil

2 pounds boneless, skinless chicken breasts or thighs (combination)

2 cups chopped onion

1 cup green bell pepper

1 cup chopped celery

2 tablespoons minced garlic

1/2 cup chopped parsley

2 teaspoons dried thyme leaves

3–4 tablespoons browned flour (see recipe in Terrific Tip)

2 1/2 cups fat-free chicken broth

16 baby potatoes

2 fresh lemon slices

1/2 cup chopped green onions

1 In large nonstick deep pan, heat oil and brown chicken on all sides, about 7–10 minutes. Remove to plate.

2 In same pan, sauté onion, green pepper, and celery until tender, about 5–7 minutes. Add garlic, parsley, thyme and browned flour, stirring. Gradually add chicken broth and bring to a boil, stirring, until flour is well-blended.

3 Lower heat and add potatoes, lemon slices and return chicken back to pan. Cook, covered, about 1 hour or until chicken is tender. Season to taste. Sprinkle with green onions when serving. Add more broth as needed.

Look for browned flour known as a roux in jars in groceries. To make: Preheat oven 400°F. Place flour on baking pan. Bake 20 minutes, stirring every 10 minutes, until dark nutty brown color.

NUTRITIONAL INFORMATION Calories 245, Calories from Fat 28%, Fat 8 g, Saturated Fat 1 g, Cholesterol 90 mg, Sodium 434 mg, Carbohydrates 18 g, Dietary Fiber 3 g, Total Sugars 3 g, Protein 26 g
DIETARY EXCHANGES 1 starch, 1 vegetable, 3 lean meat

OBESITY & DIABETES

QUICK FAVORITE FISH

Looking for a quick, moist fish recipe? Our family favorite fast fish recipe with a simple special topping makes a "hole in one" kind of dinner—perfecto!

MAKES: 4 servings · **PREP TIME:** 10 minutes · **COOK TIME:** 10–15 minutes ·

---

1 pound fish fillets (fish of choice)
2 tablespoons light mayonnaise
1 teaspoon lemon juice
1/2 teaspoon Dijon mustard
1/2 teaspoon garlic powder
1/8 teaspoon cayenne pepper
Dash Worcestershire sauce
Paprika

1 Preheat oven 500°F. Line baking pan with foil and coat with nonstick cooking spray.

2 Rinse fish fillets, and pat dry. In small dish, combine mayonnaise, lemon juice, mustard, garlic powder, cayenne pepper and Worcestershire sauce.

3 Lay fish in prepared pan. Spread mayonnaise mixture evenly over fish. Let sit 15 minutes, time permitted. Sprinkle with paprika.

4 Bake 9–14 minutes, depending on thickness of fish or until fish flakes easily with a fork.

Don't overcook fish—cook just until it begins to flake. Fish suggestions include trout, tilipia, catfish or any mild-flavored fish.

NUTRITIONAL INFORMATION Calories 102, Calories from Fat 23%, Fat 2 g, Saturated Fat 0 g, Cholesterol 46 mg, Sodium 139 mg, Carbohydrates 1 g, Dietary Fiber 0 g, Total Sugars 0 g, Protein 8 g
DIETARY EXCHANGES 3 lean meat

OVEN ROASTED SUPER SALMON

If you're trying to include more salmon in your diet, here you go with an unbeatable sweet and spicy rub for a super tasting simple salmon recipe.

MAKES: 4 servings · **PREP TIME:** 5 minutes · **COOK TIME:** 15 minutes ·

---

2 tablespoons light brown sugar

4 teaspoons chili powder

1 teaspoon ground cumin

1/4 teaspoon ground cinnamon

Salt and pepper to taste

4 (6-ounce) salmon fillets

1 Preheat oven 400°F. Coat 11×7×2-inch baking dish coated with nonstick cooking spray.

2 In small bowl, mix together brown sugar, chili powder, cumin, cinnamon and season to taste. Rub over salmon and place in prepared dish.

3 Bake 12–15 minutes or until fish flakes easily when tested with fork.

At least two servings of fish (fatty fish preferred) per week is recommended intake by the American Heart Association.

Try serving with my Quick Caesar Salad (page 86) and Roasted Honey Dijon Carrots (page 40).

NUTRITIONAL INFORMATION Calories 257, Calories from Fat 29%, Fat 8 g, Saturated Fat 1 g, Cholesterol 80 mg, Sodium 177 mg, Carbohydrates 8 g, Dietary Fiber 1 g, Total Sugars 7 g, Protein 36 g

DIETARY EXCHANGES 1/2 other carbohydrate, 5 lean meat

OBESITY & DIABETES

SIMPLE SHRIMP TACOS

Put the fabulously seasoned shrimp in the oven, make cool creamy coleslaw and combine together for an amazing simple shrimp taco. Most of the ingredients are just the seasonings!

MAKES: 8 servings · PREP TIME: 15 minutes · COOK TIME: 10 minutes ·

2 tablespoons paprika

2 tablespoons chili powder

1 tablespoon light brown sugar

1 teaspoon garlic powder

1/2 teaspoon ground cumin

1/4 teaspoon ground cinnamon

Salt and pepper to taste

2 pounds medium-large peeled shrimp

2 tablespoons olive oil

COLESLAW

2 cups shredded cabbage

1/3 cup nonfat plain Greek yogurt

1 tablespoon light mayonnaise

1 bunch green onions, chopped

1 (4-ounce) can green chiles

8 (6-inch) corn tortillas

1 Preheat oven 400°F. Line baking pan with foil and coat with nonstick cooking spray

2 In plastic zip-top resealable bag or bowl, combine all seasonings. Add shrimp and toss to coat evenly.

3 Place shrimp on prepared pan and drizzle with oil. Cook 7–9 minutes or until cooked thoroughly.

4 *For the Coleslaw:* In bowl, combine together all ingredients.

5 Assemble tacos with tortillas, shrimp and coleslaw.

Peeled shrimp may be bought fresh or frozen, if using frozen shrimp, defrost first.

Use this seasoning on fish for fantastic fish tacos. Serve with chopped avocado and tomato.

NUTRITIONAL INFORMATION Calories 203, Calories from Fat 23%, Fat 5 g, Saturated Fat 1 g, Cholesterol 184 mg, Sodium 273 mg, Carbohydrates 15 g, Dietary Fiber 4 g, Total Sugars 4 g, Protein 25 g

DIETARY EXCHANGES 1/2 starch, 1 vegetable, 3 lean meat

CRAWFISH ETOUFFEE

Crawfish Etouffee ranks high on every Louisiana menu! Here's my healthier but just as mouth-watering classic Louisiana Crawfish Etouffee recipe simmered with seasonings in a light roux. Serve over rice.

MAKES: 4 (1-cup) servings · **PREP TIME:** 10 minutes · **COOK TIME:** 25–30 minutes ·

---

2 tablespoons olive oil

3 tablespoons all-purpose flour

1 onion, chopped

1/2 cup chopped green bell pepper

1 teaspoon minced garlic

1 cup fat-free chicken broth

1 tablespoon paprika

1 pound Louisiana crawfish tails, rinsed and drained

Salt and pepper to taste

1 bunch green onions, stems only, finely chopped

1 In large nonstick skillet coated with nonstick cooking spray, heat oil and stir in flour. Cook over medium heat until light brown, about 6–8 minutes, stirring constantly. Add onion, green pepper, and garlic. Sauté until tender, about 5 minutes.

2 Gradually add broth and stir until thickened. Add paprika and bring to boil, reduce heat, cover, and cook about 5 minutes, stirring occasionally.

3 Add crawfish and continue cooking 5 more minutes or until heated. Season to taste. Top with green onions before serving.

TERRIFIC TIP

Browned flour and oil create a roux that gives the etouffee deep rich flavor.

NUGGET

Try serving with brown rice to easily boost fiber: 1 cup rice = less than 1g fiber while 1 cup brown rice = 3g fiber.

Louisiana crawfish is a high protein, low fat seafood.

NUTRITIONAL INFORMATION Calories 211, Calories from Fat 36%, Fat 8 g, Saturated Fat 1 g, Cholesterol 129 mg, Sodium 311 mg, Carbohydrates 14 g, Dietary Fiber 4 g, Total Sugars 5 g, Protein 20 g
DIETARY EXCHANGES 1/2 starch, 1 vegetable, 3 lean meat

OBESITY & DIABETES

CORNBREAD YAM DRESSING

Out of time to cook cornbread dressing and sweet potatoes?
Both holiday ingredients team up for a tasty savory stuffing or nutritious, delicious side.

MAKES: 10 (3/4 cup) servings · **PREP TIME:** 20 minutes · **COOK TIME:** 45–55 minutes ·

---

2 tablespoons canola oil

2 cups peeled sweet potato
   small chunks

1 cup chopped onion

1 cup chopped celery

1/4 cup chopped fresh parsley

1 teaspoon ground ginger

5 cups crumbled cooked cornbread

1/4 cup chopped pecans, toasted

2 tablespoons vegetable or
   chicken broth

1 Preheat oven 375°F. Coat 3-quart baking dish with nonstick cooking spray.

2 In large nonstick skillet coated with nonstick cooking spray, heat oil over medium heat. Sauté sweet potatoes, onion, and celery 7–10 minutes or until just tender, stirring.

3 Spoon mixture into large mixing bowl. Stir in parsley and ginger. Add cornbread and pecans and toss gently to coat. Add broth to moisten.

4 Place stuffing in prepared dish. Bake, uncovered, 35–45 minutes or until heated through.

 TERRIFIC **TIP**

*Time saver: buy or
prepare cornbread and
toast pecans ahead.*

 NUTRITION
NUGGET

*Sweet potatoes are
packed with vitamins
and enhance nutritional
value of this recipe.*

NUTRITIONAL INFORMATION Calories 239, Calories from Fat 33%, Fat 9 g, Saturated Fat 1 g, Cholesterol 5 mg, Sodium 341 mg, Carbohydrates 36 g, Dietary Fiber 3 g, Total Sugars 12 g, Protein 4 g
DIETARY EXCHANGES 2 1/2 starch, 1 1/2 fat

OBESITY & DIABETES

GREEK RICE

Bored with rice? Jazz it up with garlic, oregano, spinach and feta for a terrific Mediterranean rice dish.

MAKES: 6 (2/3-cup) servings · **PREP TIME:** 10 minutes · **COOK TIME:** 40–50 minutes ·

---

1 cup brown rice, uncooked

2 1/4 cups fat-free, low-sodium chicken broth

1 onion, chopped

1 teaspoon minced garlic

2 teaspoons dried oregano leaves

1 (6-ounce) bag fresh baby spinach leaves, stemmed (6 cups)

1/3 cup crumbled reduced-fat feta cheese

1 In nonstick pot, combine rice and broth. Bring to boil, stir, and reduce heat. Cover, and cook over low heat 35–45 minutes or until rice is tender.

2 Meanwhile, in large nonstick pan coated with nonstick cooking spray, sauté onion and garlic until tender. Stir in oregano and spinach, cooking only until spinach is wilted.

3 Add cooked rice, mixing well. Sprinkle with cheese.

You can always add more spinach and vegetables to recipes to boost nutrition.

I use low-sodium broth to reduce sodium for diabetic recipe.

NUTRITIONAL INFORMATION Calories 150, Calories from Fat 12%, Fat 2 g, Saturated Fat 1 g, Cholesterol 3 mg, Sodium 163 mg, Carbohydrates 28 g, Dietary Fiber 3 g, Total Sugars 2 g, Protein 6 g

DIETARY EXCHANGES 2 starch

EASY MICROWAVE OKRA

Do you like okra? May not be much to look at but this quick, tasty okra recipe is one of the easiest ever.

MAKES: 2–3 servings · **PREP TIME:** 5 minutes · **COOK TIME:** 5 minutes ·

1/2 pound whole fresh okra

3 tablespoons seasoned rice vinegar

1 tablespoon canola oil

Salt and pepper to taste

1 In shallow dish, lay okra and add vinegar and oil.

2 Microwave, covered, 4–5 minutes or until tender. Drain well and season to taste.

TERRIFIC TIP

Look for brightly colored okra without brown spots or blemishes.

NUTRITION NUGGET

Though there is no magical diabetes diet, unprocessed high fiber foods, fruits and veggies trigger less insulin release, helping control blood sugar.

NUTRITIONAL INFORMATION Calories 81, Calories from Fat 49%, Fat 5 g, Saturated Fat 0 g, Cholesterol 0 mg, Sodium 195 mg, Carbohydrates 10 g, Dietary Fiber 2 g, Total Sugars 5 g, Protein 1 g

DIETARY EXCHANGES 2 vegetable, 1 fat

ROASTED SOUTHWESTERN VEGETABLES

In my opinion, roasting leads the way to prepare vegetables for simplicity and taste.
Toss with a taco seasoning and you have a real flavor savor.

MAKES: 8 (1/2-cup) servings · **PREP TIME:** 15 minutes · **COOK TIME:** 35–40 minutes ·

4 cups peeled, cubed sweet
potatoes, cut in 1-inch cubes

1 1/2 cups zucchini, cut into small
chunks

1 cup quartered red onion slices

3 cups baby portabella
mushrooms, quartered

2 tablespoons olive oil

3 tablespoons reduced-sodium
taco seasoning mix

1 Preheat oven 425°F. Line baking pan with foil and coat with nonstick cooking spray.

2 On prepared baking pan, toss sweet potatoes, zucchini, onion, and mushrooms with olive oil to coat vegetables. Sprinkle with taco seasoning, toss.

3 Bake 35–40 minutes, turning after 20 minutes, or until vegetables are tender and roasted.

*Sweet potato and zucchini
are rich in the antioxidant,
Vitamin A, low in calories
and a good source of fiber.*

SERVING SUGGESTION

*Top salad or pasta for a new,
creative "plan-over" meal. Pop
any leftovers into a soup pot with
some chicken broth for a terrific
southwestern vegetable soup.*

NUTRITIONAL INFORMATION Calories 116, Calories from Fat 28%, Fat 4 g, Saturated Fat 1 g, Cholesterol 0 mg, Sodium 209 mg, Carbohydrates 18 g, Dietary Fiber 3 g, Total Sugars 5 g, Protein 2 g
DIETARY EXCHANGES 1 starch, 1 vegetable, 1/2 fat

OBESITY & DIABETES

PEANUT BUTTER COOKIES

My five-ingredient diabetes–friendly Peanut Butter Cookies are my #1 favorite peanut butter cookie recipe.

MAKES: 30 cookies · **PREP TIME:** 15 minutes · **COOK TIME:** 10–12 minutes ·

1 cup crunchy peanut butter
1/2 cup light brown sugar
1 egg
1/2 teaspoon baking soda
1/4 cup chopped peanuts

1 Preheat the oven 350°F. Coat baking pan with nonstick cooking spray.

2 In large bowl, combine the peanut butter, brown sugar, egg and baking soda until well combined. Stir in the peanuts.

3 Place dough by teaspoonfuls on prepared pan and press down with a fork to form ridges. Bake 10–12 minutes or until lightly browned.

Use lightly floured fork to keep from sticking to cookie batter when you make ridges in the cookies.

There's no flour in the recipe so it is gluten-free. Don't use floured fork for gluten-free version.

NUTRITIONAL INFORMATION Calories 74, Calories from Fat 58%, Fat 5 g, Saturated Fat 1 g, Cholesterol 6 mg, Sodium 59 mg, Carbohydrates 6 g, Dietary Fiber 1 g, Total Sugars 4 g, Protein 3 g
DIETARY EXCHANGES 1/2 other carbohydrate, 1 fat

ARTHRITIS & JOINT PAIN

ARTHRITIS & JOINT PAIN
THE WOUNDS OF THE WEEKEND WARRIOR

DO I HAVE ARTHRITIS OR IS THIS NORMAL JOINT PAIN?
WILL THIS PAIN EVER GO AWAY?
WHAT ARE MY OPTIONS FOR TREATMENT?

John is a 55 year old who came to see me for joint pain. He has had a very active life having played high school football and baseball. He remains active these days by playing tennis and golf; on the weekends he frequently goes to his camp where he spends most of his time repairing things. He has noticed that the joints in his hands, his knees, and his back are starting to bother him on a daily basis. The pain doesn't bother him when he is active, but at the end of the day he is in pain. Over the counter medicine helps some, but not consistently.

John's story is a very common story that I hear in my office from active men. Almost every guy has heard the term "arthritis" and they are scared to death that they may have it.

Arthritis is a very common condition—it simply means "inflamed joint." If you have long-standing joint pain, you probably have arthritis. Arthritis can be acute or chronic, involve a single joint or multiple joints. It can be one-sided or both sided. It can be caused by many different things like trauma, an immune condition, or simple wear and tear.

The most common arthritis we see in clinical practice is Osteoarthritis (OA) caused by simple wear and tear of the joints. The knees, hips and fingers are the most common joints involved; the pain tends to worsen toward the end of the day. OA can also evolve over time from trauma involving a specific joint or joints. The lumbar spine is very common place that men develop OA causing chronic low back pain.

Over the counter medications called Non-steroidal anti-inflammatory drugs (NSAIDS) like Advil or Aleve if taken periodically or chronically typically alleviate the pain associated with OA. Periodically, the pain in a single joint cannot be controlled with medication, and a more aggressive approach must be taken such as joint injection using cortisone (anti-inflammatory med) or, in severe cases—joint replacement surgery.

OA is aggravated by wear and tear; OA involving the knees and hips worsens significantly in overweight men. Studies clearly show that weight reduction is one of the best treatments for OA.

Rheumatoid Arthritis (RA) is a relatively rare arthritis that is associated with an immune system problem. The joints are more "stiff" than they are painful, and they tend to be symptomatic early in the day and improve as the day goes on. RA of the wrists and hands can be debilitating and deforming.

RA is highly treatable and managed easily if caught early. The main goal of therapy is to reduce stiffness and prevent joint deformities.

The Weekend Warrior is certainly very susceptible to developing Osteoarthritis. Over the counter therapy is readily available to help minimize pain. The most common mistake men make is not taking enough medicine for a long enough period of time; unfortunately, NSAIDS take several days to achieve maximum levels in the blood. If you have questions about what dose is appropriate, you should call your doctor.

Remedies for Joint Pain

- Weight loss
- Avoid wear and tear on the affected joint(s)
- Ice therapy to affected joint(s)
- Over the counter NSAIDs

Arthritis in its most basic definition is inflammation in the joints, which is the body's response to protect and heal itself from infection and foreign substances. It is important to reduce and prevent inflammation because chronic inflammation causes long-term tissue destruction and can lead to a host of diseases such as some cancers, heart disease, diabetes, Alzheimer's, and arthritis.

Research has shown that populations with diets rich in fruits, vegetables, nuts, healthy oils and fatty fish such as the Mediterranean diet have less chronic disease. After researching the correlation between nutrition and inflammation, I was amazed at the results. Did you know that Arthritis is the 2nd most frequently reported chronic condition with over 100 different types? Everyone can benefit from this plant based whole foods anti-inflammatory diet, and a few specific nutrients are especially important to fight against inflammation from the inside out!

Vitamin C, Vitamin A, and Omega-3 Fatty Acids

Vitamin C rich foods play an important role in tissue repair, while also helping to keep bone, cartilage and connective tissue strong in turn reducing inflammation, joint weakness and pain. Often red or orange in color, Vitamin A food (see page 107) is another antioxidant powerhouse with anti-cancer and immune boosting properties that works to combat inflammation.

Omega-3 fatty acids are essential because we must get them through food since our bodies do not make them on their own. On a cellular level, omega-3 fatty acids help regulate genetic function, blood clotting, arterial wall contraction and relaxation, and inflammation. The outcome of these protective benefits of omega-3 fatty acids include risk reduction of stroke, heart disease, arthritis, even cancer. Omega-3 supplements are popular, however the body absorbs and uses the fatty acid much better from food.

Calcium and Vitamin D

Calcium is the most abundant mineral in the body, and is required for many important metabolic, vascular and muscular functions. However, only 1% is needed for these highly regulated mineral functions, as 99% of the calcium in the body is stored in the bones making it the main nutrient for bone health. Keep your bones strong with a diet full of bone-building nutrients like calcium and vitamin D while also cutting out risk factors that leech calcium from the bones making them weak.

Foods High in Calcium:

- Dairy products—milk, cheese, yogurt, pudding
- Dark leafy greens—kale, broccoli, Chinese cabbage, bok choy
- Almonds
- Fortified cereal
- Tofu

Foods High in Vitamin D:

- Fish—salmon, tuna, mackerel
- Milk, fortified
- Orange juice, fortified
- Egg yolks
- Cereal, fortified
- Cod liver oil

Negative Bone Building Factors:

- Smoking
- Soda
- Sedentary Lifestyle

Beef Macho Nachos **PAGE 85**

BEEF MACHO NACHOS

Nutritious nachos? Don't' give up on eating peppers as the red, yellow and orange have a milder flavor. My friend, Rory, was over and doesn't usually eat peppers; he loved the nachos and begged me to heat some more up! Both the beef or chicken versions were so good, I included both recipes.

MAKES: 4 (1/2-cup) servings · **PREP TIME:** 15 minutes · **COOK TIME:** 25–30 minutes ·

1/2 pound ground sirloin

1 teaspoon minced garlic

2 teaspoons ground cumin

1/2 cup black beans, rinsed and drained

1/2 cup salsa

2 colored bell peppers, cored and cut into squares (about 12–16 per pepper)

1/2 cup shredded reduced-fat Mexican-blend cheese

1 Preheat oven 375°F. Coat baking pan with nonstick cooking spray.

2 In medium nonstick skillet, cook meat until done. Add garlic, cumin, black beans and salsa and cook for a few minutes.

3 Arrange pepper squares on baking pan. Fill with filling and sprinkle with cheese. Bake 20 minutes or until peppers crisp tender.

NUTRITIONAL INFORMATION Calories 175, Calories from Fat 32%, Fat 6 g, Saturated Fat 3 g, Cholesterol 39 mg, Sodium 344 mg, Carbohydrates 11 g, Dietary Fiber 3 g, Total Sugars 4 g, Protein 19 g

DIETARY EXCHANGES 1/2 starch, 1 vegetable, 2 1/2 lean meat

 Garnish with avocado, cilantro and dollops of sour cream.

 Bell peppers are an excellent low carb option to substitute for chips. Did you know they have more vitamin C than an orange?

BELL PEPPER CHICKEN NACHOS

MAKES: 4 (1/2-cup) servings · **PREP TIME:** 15 minutes · **COOK TIME:** 25–30 minutes ·

1 1/2 cups shredded cooked chicken breasts (rotisserie), skin removed

2 teaspoons chili powder

1/2 cup black beans, drained and rinsed

1/2 cup salsa

2 colored bell pepper, cored and cut into squares (about 12–16 per pepper)

1/2 cup shredded reduced-fat Mexican-blend cheese

1 Preheat oven 350°F. Coat baking pan with nonstick cooking spray.

2 In bowl, combine chicken, chili powder, black beans and salsa.

3 Arrange pepper squares on baking pan. Fill with filling and sprinkle with cheese. Bake 20 minutes or until peppers crisp tender.

NUTRITIONAL INFORMATION Calories 178, Calories from Fat 26%, Fat 5 g, Saturated Fat 2 g, Cholesterol 55 mg, Sodium 503 mg, Carbohydrates 11 g, Dietary Fiber 3 g, Total Sugars 3 g, Protein 22 g

DIETARY EXCHANGES 1/2 starch, 1 vegetable, 2 1/2 lean meat

QUICK CAESAR SALAD

Enjoy my popular, unpretentious version of this classic crisp salad—perfect starter to any meal.

MAKES: About 4 heaping (1-cup) servings · **PREP TIME:** 5 minutes · **COOK TIME:** None ·

1 large head romaine lettuce, torn into pieces (about 8 cups)

1/4 cup grated Parmesan cheese

1 tablespoon sesame seeds

1/2 cup nonfat plain Greek yogurt

1/2 teaspoon minced garlic

2 tablespoons lemon juice

1 teaspoon vinegar

1 teaspoon Worcestershire sauce

1 teaspoon Dijon mustard

1 In large bowl, combine lettuce, cheese and sesame seeds.

2 In small bowl, whisk together remaining ingredients. Toss with lettuce.

SERVING SUGGESTION

Make it an entree salad by topping with Grilled Chicken or Shrimp (page 170).

TERRIFIC TIP

Think about adding veggies to your salad for added nutrition.

NUTRITION NUGGET

Did you know that sesame seeds are a great source of calcium?

NUTRITIONAL INFORMATION Calories 73, Calories from Fat 38%, Fat 3 g, Saturated Fat 1 g, Cholesterol 4 mg, Sodium 135 mg, Carbohydrates 6 g, Dietary Fiber 2 g, Total Sugars 3 g, Protein 6 g

DIETARY EXCHANGES 1 vegetable, 1/2 lean meat

WATERMELON AND CANTALOUPE SALAD

Melons with honey, mint, basil, and feta reward you with a fresh, fast salad with benefits.
Did you know that watermelon is hydrating and helps with muscle recovery?

MAKES: 6 (1/2-cup) servings · **PREP TIME:** 5 minutes · **COOK TIME:** None ·

2 cups watermelon small chunks
or balls

1 cup cantaloupe small chunks
or balls

2 tablespoons lemon juice

2 tablespoons honey

2 tablespoons chopped fresh mint

2 teaspoons dried basil leaves or
1 teaspoon chopped fresh basil

Salt and pepper to taste

1/4 cup crumbled reduced-fat feta
cheese

1 In large bowl, combine watermelon and cantaloupe.

2 In small bowl, mix together lemon juice, honey, mint and basil. Season to taste.

3 Toss with watermelon mixture. Refrigerate until serving. Add feta before serving.

*Make this salad the
night before for flavors
to meld together.*

*This salad packs immune-
boosting carotenoid
antioxidants found in
watermelon and cantaloupe.*

NUTRITIONAL INFORMATION Calories 60 kcal, Calories from fat 11%, Fat 1 g, Saturated Fat 0 g, Cholesterol 2 mg, Sodium 89 mg, Carbohydrates 13 g, Dietary Fiber 1 g, Total Sugars 11 g, Protein 2 g

DIETARY EXCHANGES 1 fruit

CARIBBEAN BLACK BEAN AND MANGO SALAD

Five heart healthy packed ingredients in a colorful, refreshing tropical salad with a zingy vinaigrette is rich in healthy weight maintaining fiber helping keep you full and satisfied.

MAKES: about 8 (1/2-cup) servings · **PREP TIME:** 10 minutes · **COOK TIME:** None ·

---

1 (15-ounce) can black beans, rinsed and drained

1 cup chopped mango

1/2 cup chopped red onion

1 avocado, chopped

2 tablespoons lime juice

1 teaspoon light brown sugar

1/2 teaspoon ground ginger

1 In medium bowl, combine all ingredients. Refrigerate until serving.

Save a step and buy sliced fresh mango or look for in jars, cans or frozen in the grocery.

Mangos are loaded with the antioxidant, Vitamin C, helping to boost the immune system.

NUTRITIONAL INFORMATION Calories 105, Calories from Fat 35%, Fat 4 g, Saturated Fat 1 g, Cholesterol 0 mg, Sodium 153 mg, Carbohydrates 14 g, Dietary Fiber 5 g, Total Sugars 4 g, Protein 4 g
DIETARY EXCHANGES 1/2 starch, 1/2 fruit, 1 fat

SOUTHWESTERN VEGGIE QUINOA BOWL

This fabulous vegetarian southwestern quinoa recipe will be a game changer for you. Put quinoa on to cook, sauté vegetables and combine to pop in the oven for a hearty, healthy and wonderful one-dish quick meal!

MAKES: 6 (1-cup) servings · **PREP TIME:** 15 minutes · **COOK TIME:** 45 minutes ·

3/4 cup quinoa

1 1/2 cups water

1 cup chopped onion

1 red bell pepper, cored and chopped

1 cup chopped peeled sweet potato

1 teaspoon minced garlic

1 teaspoon ground chili powder

1 teaspoon ground oregano

1/2 teaspoon ground cumin

1 (15-ounce) can black beans, rinsed and drained

1 1/2 cups salsa

1/4 cup fresh chopped cilantro

1 cup shredded reduced-fat Mexican-blend cheese

1 Preheat oven 350°F. Coat 9-inch baking dish with nonstick cooking spray.

2 In medium nonstick pot, combine quinoa and water. Bring to boil, reduce heat and cook, covered about 17–20 minutes or until water absorbed and quinoa cooked. Remove from heat and fluff with fork. Set aside.

3 Meanwhile, in large nonstick pan coated with nonstick cooking spray, sauté onion, bell pepper, sweet potato, and garlic until tender, about 5–7 minutes. Add chili powder, oregano, and cumin.

4 Combine vegetables with cooked quinoa, black beans, salsa, and cilantro. Transfer to prepared baking dish. Top with cheese. Bake 20 minutes or until cheese is melted.

Chicken may be added if you want a heartier meal. Garnish with diced avocado, and tomatoes.

NUTRITIONAL INFORMATION Calories 250, Calories from Fat 21%, Fat 6 g, Saturated Fat 2 g, Cholesterol 12 mg, Sodium 600 mg, Carbohydrates 36 g, Dietary Fiber 7 g, Total Sugars 6 g, Protein 12 g

DIETARY EXCHANGES 1 vegetable, 2 starch, 1 lean meat

BUTTERNUT SQUASH, KALE AND CRANBERRY COUSCOUS

Touch down worthy—get festive with this colorful combination of sweet butternut squash, crunchy kale, tart cranberries and toasty walnuts. You'll love the versatility to serve it hot, room temperature or cold.

MAKES: 6 (1-cup) servings · **PREP TIME:** 15 minutes · **COOK TIME:** 30 minutes ·

---

4 cups cubed butternut squash

Salt and pepper to taste

1 cup pearl couscous, cooked in water according to package instructions

2 cups coarsely chopped kale leaves

3 tablespoons dried cranberries

1/4 cup chopped walnuts, toasted

2 ounces crumbled goat cheese, optional

ORANGE VINAIGRETTE

2 tablespoons apple cider vinegar

1 tablespoon olive oil

3 tablespoons orange juice

1 Preheat oven 425°F. Line baking pan with foil and coat with nonstick cooking spray.

2 Arrange squash on prepared pan. Season to taste and coat with nonstick cooking spray. Bake 15 minutes, stir, and continue cooking 10–15 minutes or until squash is tender.

3 Remove from oven and transfer to large bowl. Add cooked couscous, kale, cranberries, walnuts, and goat cheese, if desired.

4 *For the Orange Vinaigrette:* Whisk together ingredients until mixed. Toss with couscous mixture.

With pre-cut butternut squash, chopped kale, and quick cooking couscous, this salad comes together quickly.

You know you are eating with nutrition with this colorful of a plate—each color providing important protective vitamins and nutrients to reduce aches and joint pain.

NUTRITIONAL INFORMATION Calories 230, Calories from Fat 22%, Fat 6 g, Saturated Fat 1 g, Cholesterol 0 mg, Sodium 16 mg, Carbohydrates 40 g, Dietary Fiber 4 g, Total Sugars 5 g, Protein 6 g

DIETARY EXCHANGES 2 1/2 starch, 1 fat

CHICKEN PASTA PRIMAVERA

You'll get bragging rights when you make this one-dish meal with chicken, bell peppers, tomatoes and spinach in a quick light creamy Alfredo-style sauce.

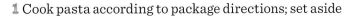

MAKES: 6 (1 1/3-cup) servings · **PREP TIME:** 15 minutes · **COOK TIME:** 20–25 minutes ·

8 ounces linguine

1 1/4 pounds chicken breasts, cut into small strips

Salt and pepper to taste

2 assorted colored bell peppers, cored and thinly sliced

1/2 red onion, sliced

1 tablespoon minced garlic

2 cups chopped tomatoes

1/3 cup skim milk

2 tablespoons all-purpose flour

3 tablespoons reduced-fat cream cheese

1 cup fat-free chicken broth

2 cups fresh baby spinach leaves

1 Cook pasta according to package directions; set aside

2 Season chicken to taste. In large nonstick skillet coated with nonstick cooking spray, cook chicken over medium-high heat until almost done, about 7 minutes.

3 Add bell peppers and onion to skillet, sauté 3–5 minutes until crisp tender. Add garlic and tomatoes and sauté 3–4 more minutes or until vegetables are tender.

4 In small bowl, whisk together milk, flour and cream cheese. Add milk mixture and broth to pan, stirring, and bring to a boil. Reduce heat and cook about 2 minutes. Add spinach and linguine; toss until well heated.

NUTRITION NUGGET

Bell peppers have more Vitamin C than an orange which plays an important role in growth and tissue repair—helping to relieve arthritis inflammation and pain.

TERRIFIC TIP

Drained canned tomatoes may be substituted for fresh tomatoes.

NUTRITIONAL INFORMATION Calories 308, Calories from Fat 15%, Fat 5 g, Saturated Fat 2 g, Cholesterol 66 mg, Sodium 316 mg, Carbohydrates 37 g, Dietary Fiber 3 g, Total Sugars 5 g, Protein 28 g

DIETARY EXCHANGES 2 starch, 1 vegetable, 3 lean meat

CHICKEN IN SPICY PEANUT BUTTER SAUCE

Why get take-out when you can excite your taste buds with this exceptional stir-fry in a spicy sauce.
Don't let the long ingredient list scare you—look for sliced peppers, shredded carrots and shelled edamame.

MAKES: 5 (1-cup) servings · PREP TIME: 15 minutes · COOK TIME: 20 minutes ·

1 tablespoon canola oil

1 teaspoon minced garlic

2 tablespoons grated fresh ginger

1/2 teaspoon red pepper flakes

1 1/2 pounds thin boneless chicken breasts, cut into thin strips

1 cup finely sliced red bell pepper

1 cup shredded or chopped carrots

1 cup frozen shelled edamame

Spicy Peanut Butter Sauce (see recipe below)

1/2 cup chopped green onions

1 In large nonstick skillet, heat oil over medium-high heat. Add garlic, ginger and red pepper flakes; stir fry 1 minute. Add chicken and cook, stirring, until chicken is done, about 5 minutes.

2 Add sliced red pepper, carrots and edamame. Stir-fry about 5 minutes or until vegetables are tender.

3 Add Spicy Peanut Butter Sauce to skillet; cooking until peanut butter melts. Sprinkle with green onions.

High protein ingredients like chicken, edamame and peanut butter plus antioxidant bell peppers make this a healthy choice.

Serve over rice or rice noodles.

If Spicy Peanut Butter Sauce is too thick, add more water.

SPICY PEANUT BUTTER SAUCE

The secret is in the sauce!

1/4 cup peanut butter

2 tablespoons low-sodium soy sauce

1 tablespoon sesame oil

1 tablespoon seasoned rice vinegar

1/4 cup hot water

1 In small bowl, combine all ingredients.

NUTRITIONAL INFORMATION Calories 356, Calories from Fat 43%, Fat 17 g, Saturated Fat 3 g, Cholesterol 87 mg, Sodium 439 mg, Carbohydrates 13 g, Dietary Fiber 4 g, Total Sugars 7 g, Protein 37 g
DIETARY EXCHANGES 1/2 starch, 1 vegetable, 4 lean meat, 1 fat

CURRY CHICKEN

Change up chicken with this super-satisfying and super easy recipe with only a few pantry-friendly ingredients you probably already have on hand like mustard, honey and curry.

MAKES: 4 servings · PREP TIME: 5 minutes · COOK TIME: 30–35 minutes ·

1 tablespoon olive oil

1/4 cup Dijon mustard

3 tablespoons honey

1/2 teaspoon ground curry powder

1 1/2 pounds skinless, boneless
    thin chicken breasts

1 Preheat oven 350°F. Line baking pan with foil and coat with nonstick cooking spray.

2 In bowl, blend oil, mustard, honey and curry. Arrange chicken on baking pan. Pour sauce over chicken, coating chicken.

3 Bake 30–35 minutes or until chicken is done.

Use chicken breasts or thighs.

Curry has ingredients that have been found to have anti-inflammatory properties helping to reduce arthritic pain.

NUTRITIONAL INFORMATION Calories 292, Calories from Fat 28%, Fat 9 g, Saturated Fat 1 g, Cholesterol 109 mg, Sodium 505 mg, Carbohydrates 16 g, Dietary Fiber 1 g, Total Sugars 14 g, Protein 37 g

DIETARY EXCHANGES 1 starch, 5 lean meat

SALSA CHICKEN

Salsa and southwestern seasoning with healthy Vitamin C packed red pepper and fiber-rich black beans collide with flavors for a speedy and spectacular chicken recipe.

MAKES: 6 servings · PREP TIME: 10 minutes · COOK TIME: 1 hour · F G

2 pounds chicken tenders

2 cups salsa

1 red bell pepper, cored and chopped

1 tablespoon ground cumin

1 tablespoon chili powder

1 tablespoon minced garlic

1 (15-ounce) can black beans, drained and rinsed

Optional toppings: Condiments, chopped avocado, cheese, green onions

1 Preheat oven 400°F. Coat 3-quart baking dish with nonstick cooking spray.

2 Lay chicken tenders in baking dish.

3 In bowl, combine salsa, bell pepper, cumin, chili powder and garlic. Spread over chicken and top with black beans.

4 Bake, covered with foil, 1 hour or until chicken is tender.

NUTRITION NUGGET

Did you know that 1/2 cup of salsa equals one serving of vegetables?

SERVING SUGGESTION

Serve topped with condiments over rice as entrée or wrap up in tortillas with condiments for a wrap.

NUTRITIONAL INFORMATION Calories 275, Calories from Fat 17%, Fat 5 g, Saturated Fat 1 g, Cholesterol 97 mg, Sodium 70 mg, Carbohydrates 7 g, Dietary Fiber 5 g, Total Sugars 4 g, Protein 37 g

DIETARY EXCHANGES 1/2 starch, 1 vegetable, 4 lean meat

SAUSAGE AND ROASTED PEPPERS

Roasted antioxidant-rich bell peppers pack a powerful punch when combined
with sausage for a high scoring delicious recipe.

MAKES: 8 (1-cup) servings · PREP TIME: 15 minutes · COOK TIME: 45–55 minutes ·

6 cups assorted bell peppers,
cored and cut into small squares

1 cup chopped onion

1 tablespoon minced garlic

1 pound turkey sausage

1 (14 1/2-ounce) can fire roasted
tomatoes

2 cups fat-free chicken broth

1 tablespoon dried basil leaves

4 cups fresh baby spinach leaves

1 Preheat oven 425°F. Coat baking pan with foil and nonstick cooking spray.

2 Spread peppers evenly on foil lined pan and roast 30–40 minutes until tender and lightly browned.

3 Meanwhile, in large nonstick skillet, cook onion, garlic and sausage until sausage is done, about 5–7 minutes. Add tomatoes, roasted peppers, broth and basil.

4 Bring to boil, lower heat and cook about 10 minutes. Add spinach and stir until wilted.

*For the turkey sausage, you
can substitute ground turkey,
ground sirloin or Italian
Chicken Sausage.*

*I served it over pasta
but you can serve over
couscous, quinoa or rice.*

NUTRITIONAL INFORMATION Calories 157, Calories from Fat 35%, Fat 6 g, Saturated Fat 2 g, Cholesterol 48 mg, Sodium 779 mg, Carbohydrates 14 g, Dietary Fiber 4 g, Total Sugars 8 g, Protein 11 g

DIETARY EXCHANGES 3 vegetable, 1 lean meat

ARTHRITIS & JOINT PAIN

HONEY PECAN SALMON

Take salmon up a notch with this amazing honey pecan topping.
It was so delicious I forgot I was eating a good-for-you fish!

MAKES: 4 servings · PREP TIME: 5 minutes · COOK TIME: 12–15 minutes ·

1/4 cup honey

1 tablespoon finely chopped pecans

1 tablespoon low-sodium soy sauce

4 (6-ounce) salmon fillets

1 Combine honey, pecans and soy sauce in large plastic zip-top resealable bag or dish. Add salmon and marinate in refrigerator 15 minutes or time permitted.

2 Preheat oven 425°F. Line baking pan with foil and coat with nonstick cooking spray.

3 Place salmon on pan and top with marinade and pecans, reserving remaining marinade. Bake 12–15 minutes or until salmon flakes easily with fork, baste salmon halfway through with marinade and then discard any remaining marinade.

Think of salmon as a high protein food and this recipe fuels your muscles without compromising taste!

NUTRITIONAL INFORMATION Calories 267, Calories from Fat 30%, Fat 9 g, Saturated Fat 2 g, Cholesterol 80 mg, Sodium 228 mg, Carbohydrates 9 g, Dietary Fiber 0 g, Total Sugars 9 g, Protein 36 g

DIETARY EXCHANGES 1/2 other carbohydrate, 5 lean meat

SALMON MARSALA

Fancy flair without the fuss but you will leave a lasting impression—Marsala wine gives this quick cooking salmon recipe a sophisticated flavor.

MAKES: 4 servings · PREP TIME: 10 minutes · COOK TIME: 10 minutes ·

1 tablespoons olive oil
1 medium onion, thinly sliced
1 teaspoon minced garlic
1/2 pound sliced mushrooms
4 (4-ounce) skinless salmon fillets
1/3 cup Marsala wine
3/4 cup fat-free chicken broth
3 teaspoons cornstarch

1 In large nonstick skillet, heat oil and sauté onion, garlic, and mushrooms until tender.

2 Add salmon to skillet, cooking 4 minutes, turn onto other side. Meanwhile, in small bowl, mix together wine, broth and cornstarch.

3 When salmon is almost done, add wine mixture to the salmon. Stir gently, as mixture thickens quickly.

NUTRITION NUGGET

Omega-3 fatty acids play an important role in our health, from reducing the risk of heart disease and stroke, lowering cholesterol, to reducing joint pain from inflammation. We must get omega-3 fatty acids through diet as they are not made in the body and salmon is a rich source.

SERVING SUGGESTION

Serve with Quick Caesar Salad (page 86).

NUTRITIONAL INFORMATION Calories 244, Calories from Fat 32%, Fat 9 g, Saturated Fat 1 g, Cholesterol 53 mg, Sodium 267 mg, Carbohydrates 10 g, Dietary Fiber 1 g, Total Sugars 5 g, Protein 26 g
DIETARY EXCHANGES 1 vegetable, 1/2 other carbohydrate, 3 lean meat

ARTHRITIS & JOINT PAIN

UNSTUFFED BELL PEPPER CASSEROLE

A slam dunk recipe for stuffed peppers because you get the full-flavored ingredients of a stuffed pepper without the hassle of stuffing them in this delicious one-dish meal.

MAKES: 8 servings · PREP TIME: 15 minutes · COOK TIME: 35–40 minutes ·

1 pound ground sirloin

1/2 cup chopped onion

2 cups chopped red, green and yellow bell peppers

1 teaspoon minced garlic

Salt and pepper to taste

1 (14 1/2-ounce) can fire-roasted diced tomatoes

1 1/2 cups instant rice, uncooked (try brown rice)

1 tablespoon Worcestershire sauce

1 teaspoon dried basil leaves

1 teaspoon dried oregano leaves

1 1/3 cups shredded reduced-fat sharp Cheddar cheese, divided

1 (15-ounce) can tomato sauce

1 Preheat oven 375°F. Coat 13×9×2-inch baking dish with nonstick cooking spray.

2 In large nonstick skillet, cook meat, onion, peppers and garlic 7–10 minutes or until meat is browned. Drain excess fat, and season to taste. Stir in tomatoes, uncooked rice, Worcestershire sauce, basil and oregano.

3 Remove from heat, add 2/3 cup cheese, stirring to combine. Transfer to prepared dish. Spread with tomato sauce. Bake 20–25 minutes, uncovered, or until rice is cooked. Sprinkle with remaining cheese and return to oven 5 minutes or until cheese is melted.

Substitute ground turkey for ground sirloin, if desired. If using instant brown rice, it takes longer to cook.

NUTRITIONAL INFORMATION Calories 240, Calories from Fat 26%, Fat 7 g, Saturated Fat 3 g, Cholesterol 41 mg, Sodium 613 mg, Carbohydrates 23 g, Dietary Fiber 3 g, Total Sugars 6 g, Protein 21 g
DIETARY EXCHANGES 1 starch, 2 vegetable, 2 1/2 lean meat

CREAMY MAC AND CHEESE

My classic creamy mac and cheese comes out even better, faster, and creamier than the kind out of the box.

MAKES: 9 (2/3-cup) servings · **PREP TIME:** 5 minutes · **COOK TIME:** 10 minutes ·

8 ounces small macaroni

2 tablespoons cornstarch

2 cups skim milk

6 slices reduced-fat American cheese

1 cup shredded reduced-fat Cheddar cheese

Salt and pepper to taste

1 Cook macaroni according to package directions. Drain well and set aside.

2 In large nonstick pot, mix cornstarch and milk and bring to a boil. Lower heat, stirring, and cook until thickened, about 5 minutes.

3 Reduce heat and add American cheese and Cheddar cheese, stirring until melted. Add macaroni; mixing well. Season to taste.

Try adding veggies to your mac and cheese to boost nutrition.

Calcium is the most abundant mineral in the body and is important for bone health.

Good calcium sources include dairy products like milk and yogurt, and dark leafy greens such as kale and broccoli.

NUTRITIONAL INFORMATION Calories 193, Calories from Fat 25%, Fat 5 g, Saturated Fat 3 g, Cholesterol 17 mg, Sodium 281 mg, Carbohydrates 24 g, Dietary Fiber 1 g, Total Sugars 4 g, Protein 12 g

DIETARY EXCHANGES 1 1/2 starch, 1/2 fat

PIZZA RICE

This five-ingredient pizza-inspired rice with Italian cheesy flavors is a team player that goes with any meal.

MAKES: 6 (3/4 cup) servings · **PREP TIME:** 5 minutes · **COOK TIME:** 10 minutes ·

1 small green bell pepper, chopped

1 (14 1/2-ounce) can diced fire-roasted tomatoes with juice

1 (.7-ounce) package Italian salad dressing mix

4 cups cooked brown rice

1 cup shredded part-skim mozzarella cheese

1 In a medium nonstick pot coated with nonstick cooking spray, sauté green pepper until tender. Add tomatoes and Italian dressing, stirring until mixed and well heated.

2 Stir in the cooked rice, and cheese. Cook over low heat until well heated and cheese melted, 3–5 minutes.

Turn leftover cooked rice into another delicious rice recipe.

Did you know 1 cup brown rice has 3 1/2 grams fiber and white rice has less than one gram?

NUTRITIONAL INFORMATION Calories 216, Calories from Fat 18%, Fat 4 g, Saturated Fat 2 g, Cholesterol 12 mg, Sodium 761 mg, Carbohydrates 36 g, Dietary Fiber 4 g, Total Sugars 5 g, Protein 9 g

DIETARY EXCHANGES 2 starch, 1 vegetable, 1/2 lean meat

BROCCOLI WITH WALNUTS

Turn on your stovetop and stir-fry broccoli, with walnuts, a hint of heat,
and Parmesan cheese for a dazzling veggie.

MAKES: 8 (1-cup) servings · **PREP TIME:** 5 minutes · **COOK TIME:** 10 minutes ·

---

2 tablespoons olive oil

10 cups broccoli florets

Salt and pepper to taste

1 teaspoon minced garlic

1/3 cup coarsely chopped walnuts

2 tablespoons lemon juice

1/4 teaspoon red pepper flakes

3 tablespoons grated Parmesan
cheese

1 In large nonstick skillet, heat oil and cook broccoli over medium-high heat, stirring until begins to get tender. Season to taste.

2 Add garlic and walnuts; cook until broccoli is crisp tender and walnuts are toasted. Toss with lemon juice, red pepper flakes and Parmesan.

Fiber packed broccoli and omega-3 fatty acid rich walnuts make this a high antioxidant recipe.

Turn this delicious broccoli side into a vegetarian meal by tossing with pasta or your favorite grain.

NUTRITIONAL INFORMATION Calories 111, Calories from Fat 56%, Fat 8 g, Saturated Fat 1 g, Cholesterol 2 mg, Sodium 67 mg, Carbohydrates 9 g, Dietary Fiber 3 g, Total Sugars 2 g, Protein 5 g

DIETARY EXCHANGES 2 vegetable, 1 1/2 fat

SESAME ASPARAGUS OR GREEN BEANS

Asparagus or green beans dazzle in taste when tossed with ginger
and sesame seeds for a nutritious no-fuss side dish.

MAKES: About 2–3 servings · **PREP TIME:** 5 minutes · **COOK TIME:** 5–7 minutes ·

3/4 pound fresh asparagus spears
   or 3/4 pound green beans,
   ends snapped

1 teaspoon minced garlic

1 teaspoon minced fresh ginger or
   1/2 teaspoon ground ginger

2 teaspoons sesame oil

1 tablespoon low-sodium soy sauce

1 teaspoon toasted sesame seeds

1 In large nonstick skillet coated with nonstick cooking spray, stir-fry asparagus or green beans over medium heat about 4–6 minutes, until crisp tender.

2 Add garlic, ginger, oil and soy sauce and cook until heated. Sprinkle with sesame seeds.

TERRIFIC

To toast sesame seeds, place on baking pan and toast in 350°F oven about 5–7 minutes. Watch carefully, as they burn easily. Or buy toasted sesame seeds in spice aisle or Asian food section of supermarket.

NUTRITION NUGGET

Did you know small little sesame seeds are full of bone-building calcium? Per tablespoon, whole sesame seeds contain about 88 mg of calcium.

NUTRITIONAL INFORMATION Calories 46, Calories from Fat 50%, Fat 3 g, Saturated Fat 0 g, Cholesterol 0 mg, Sodium 100 mg, Carbohydrates 4 g, Dietary Fiber 2 g, Total Sugars 2 g, Protein 2 g
DIETARY EXCHANGES 1 vegetable, 1/2 fat

CANDIED WALNUTS

Craving sweet and spice and everything nice—I'm talking about these wonderful walnuts.
A handful of mixed nuts fills you up!

MAKES: 8 (1/4 cup) servings · **PREP TIME:** 5 minutes · **COOK TIME:** 5–7 minutes ·

2 cups walnut halves

1 tablespoon sugar

1/4 teaspoon salt

1/2 teaspoon garlic powder

1/2 teaspoon ground cumin

1/4 teaspoon ground cinnamon

1/4 teaspoon cayenne pepper

1 tablespoon canola oil

1 Preheat oven 375°F.

2 Spread walnuts on baking sheet. Bake about 5–7 minutes or until golden.

3 In small bowl, combine sugar, salt, garlic powder, cumin, cinnamon, and cayenne pepper.

4 In nonstick skillet, heat oil over medium heat. Add nuts and stir to coat with oil. Add seasoning mix, stirring until nuts coated. Remove nuts to paper towel to cool.

You can also use pecans which are high in antioxidants.

Walnuts are rich in anti-inflammatory omega-3 fatty acids.

Toss in salads, serve on cheese trays or as snack.

NUTRITIONAL INFORMATION Calories 187, Calories from Fat 82%, Fat 18 g, Saturated Fat 2 g, Cholesterol 0 mg, Sodium 74 mg, Carbohydrates 5 g, Dietary Fiber 2 g, Total Sugars 2 g, Protein 4 g
DIETARY EXCHANGES 1/2 other carbohydrate, 3 1/2 fat

NO-BAKE CHOCOLATE OATMEAL PEANUT BUTTER BARS

Slam dunk favorite for grab and go bars with oatmeal, peanut butter and chocolate.
Quick snack, dessert or breakfast on the run.

MAKES: 36 bars · **PREP TIME:** 5 minutes · **COOK TIME:** 2–5 minutes ·

---

1 cup sugar

1/4 cup cocoa

1/2 cup butter

1/2 cup skim milk

3 1/2 cups old-fashioned oatmeal

1/2 cup creamy peanut butter

1 teaspoon vanilla extract

1 Coat 13×9×2-inch baking pan with nonstick cooking spray.

2 In large nonstick pot, heat sugar, cocoa, butter and milk, stirring until dissolved. Bring mixture to boil, and boil 2 minutes.

3 Remove from heat. Stir in oatmeal, peanut butter and vanilla until well combined. Transfer to prepared pan. Refrigerate at least 4 hours or until hardened. Cut into squares.

Oatmeal is a slow digesting carb that helps suppress hunger.

NUTRITIONAL INFORMATION Calories 98, Calories from Fat 44%, Fat 5 g, Saturated Fat 2 g, Cholesterol 7 mg, Sodium 41 mg, Carbohydrates 12 g, Dietary Fiber 1 g, Total Sugars 6 g, Protein 2 g
DIETARY EXCHANGES 1 other carbohydrate, 1 fat

CANCER

CANCER
THE HIDDEN SNIPER

WHAT ARE RISK FACTORS AND SYMPTOMS OF LUNG, COLON, SKIN AND PROSTATE CANCER?
ARE THERE TESTS OR SCREENINGS I SHOULD BE DOING?
HOW CAN I REDUCE MY CHANCES OF GETTING CANCER?

I've always thought of cancer as a hidden sniper, hiding out of sight, just waiting for an opportunity to take a fatal shot at me when I least expect it. My defense as a man and as a physician has become— find the sniper before he has a chance to find me, or one of my patients.

Approximately 80% of all cancer deaths in men are caused by only four cancers: lung cancer, colon cancer, skin cancer, and prostate cancer. Let's talk about each one.

Lung Cancer

- Strong association with Tobacco use
- Typically identified on chest x-ray, but usually too late to be cured
- Screen for lung cancer by using high resolution CT scan in at-risk individuals. Small cancers can be detected which are more likely to be curable.

Colon Cancer

- A family history of colon cancer is a strong risk factor
- Symptoms may include blood in stool, intestinal obstruction, unexplained low blood count
- Rarely symptomatic until cancer is in advanced stages
- Screen for colon cancer using colonoscopy or other stool testing
- Unfortunately, 30% of men choose to never have colon cancer screening

Skin Cancer

- Skin cancer is the most common cancer in the US.
- Melanoma is a deadly form of skin cancer that spreads throughout the body
- Early detection of melanoma is critical to survival.
- Screen for melanoma and other skin cancers by having annual full-body skin evaluation by your primary care physician or dermatologist

Prostate Cancer

- Prostate cancer is the second most common cancer in men.
- Symptoms of prostate cancer are rare, but may include difficult or painful urination, blood in the urine, or painful ejaculation.
- Very curable if caught early. If caught late, cure is more difficult.
- Screen for prostate cancer with a blood test (prostate specific antigen) and an annual digital rectal exam by a trained clinician.

The Ugly Truth About Cancer Screening

Let's get it out on the table—two of the three screening tests for the most common cancers in men involve getting something stuck up their hind end. That's why many men choose to ignore these important tests and just "hope for the best." I can't begin to tell you what a mistake that can be.

The course of illness associated with colon cancer and prostate cancer can be a very traumatic not only for the patient but also for the entire family. The clinical problems associated with these two cancers can be unpredictable and severe. Additionally, the resources required to care for a loved one are expensive, and this can be financially catastrophic for a family. In short, you don't want any part of either of these two snipers.

I remember a 52 year-old man who year after year would refuse to have a colonoscopy. He would proudly proclaim that he "would never have anything shoved up his butt." Five years later, he came to the ER with stomach pain. A quick CT scan confirmed the worst: an obstructing colon cancer which had spread to the liver. He looked at me and I looked at him. He didn't say a word, but I knew what he was thinking. He knew he had messed up. All he said to me was, "Tell my family that I'm sorry."

Look—no man wants to have anything stuck up his hind end, I get it. Having personally experienced both of these tests on several occasions, the truth is that both of these screening tests, colonoscopy and digital rectal exam, are completely painless. And a colonoscopy is performed while you're sound asleep! In fact, one of the best naps I've ever had is during a colonoscopy.

Role of Nutrition in Cancer Prevention

Did you know that 35% of all cancer have some nutritional relationship and 1.7 million people yearly are diagnosed with cancer? We know food is an important part of staying healthy and avoiding disease, and there is not one food or food group that is most important to preventing and surviving cancer. A healthy balanced diet within moderation, and according to the USDA Dietary Guidelines, is the best recommendation for food intake; however there are a few stand-out foods that have been shown to help lower that risk.

High Fiber, Vitamin C and Vitamin A

It's true what you learned as a kid, fruits and vegetables really are good for you for seemingly limitless reasons. Most notably their fiber, vitamin and mineral content which are necessary for our body's everyday functions but also act as

antioxidants inhibiting cancerous cell production. Healthy foods high in fiber have been shown to protect against colon cancer. Risk of bladder, prostate, stomach, esophageal, and lung cancer is shown to be lowered with a diet high in fruits and vegetables.

Cruciferous vegetables have been shown to reduce the risk of cancer. Vitamin C-rich foods protect against cancer of the mouth, esophagus, pancreas and stomach. Carotenoids (phytonutrients that turn into Vitamin A in the body) are powerful antioxidants with anti-cancer, anti-oxidant, and immune boosting properties. They often give fruit and vegetables their red, orange, or yellow color.

Foods High in Fiber:
- Whole grains
- Fruits
- Vegetables
- Legumes

Cruciferous Vegetables:
- Kale
- Cauliflower
- Broccoli

Foods High in Vitamin C:
- Bell peppers, red, yellow and green
- Oranges
- Kale
- Spinach
- Broccoli
- Strawberries
- Pineapple
- Melons
- Fortified cereals

Foods High in Vitamin A:
- Sweet potatoes
- Tomatoes
- Carrots
- Brussels sprouts
- Spinach
- Broccoli

What Foods To Avoid

Fats Aren't Created Equal

Perhaps as important as what to include in your diet is what to leave out. There is good evidence that fat increases your risk of developing cancer, especially cancer of the prostate, colon, breast, ovary, endometrium, and pancreas. However, all fat is not created equal with saturated and trans fat being more likely to increase your risk for cancer.

The *2015–2020 Dietary Guidelines for Americans* recommend saturated fat intake should be limited to less than 10 percent of calories per day and they should be replaced with unsaturated fats. They also recommend trans-fat intake should be as low as possible. Research shows that increased intake of trans-fats is linked to increased risk of cardiovascular disease.

Unsaturated fat is the healthy fat and comes in two forms: monounsaturated and polyunsaturated. The body needs a moderate amount of healthy fat to function and research shows that within a well-balanced diet, unsaturated fats can lower cholesterol levels and help prevent heart disease. All fat, even healthy unsaturated fat should be eaten in moderation for weight maintenance as it is calorie dense.

Unsaturated Fat Sources: peanut butter, avocado, raw nuts, fish (salmon, halibut, tuna), olive oil, canola oil

Saturated Fat Sources: fatty beef, poultry with skin, butter, cheese, whole milk,

Trans Fat Sources: biscuits, especially flakey and frozen biscuits, cakes and pies, frosting, margarine, crackers, doughnuts, fried fast foods, frozen pizza

Easy Substitutions To Swap For Better Health

- Choose reduced-fat dairy products (cheese, milk, ice cream)
- Choose meat with "loin" or "round" in the name—for example: ground sirloin
- Add extra veggies to sauces, stews or casseroles
- Forget the chips, and dip with fresh veggies
- Bake with less sugar
- Eat skinless chicken or turkey breasts
- Replace meat with nutrient rich protein (beans, chicken, fish or shrimp)
- Substitute 2 egg whites for 1 egg in recipes
- Use oil-based condiments instead of those made with solid fats (such as butter, cream cheese)
- For sour cream, use nonfat plain Greek yogurt

TOMATO BRUSCHETTA

Fresh tomatoes, basil and a few ingredients make this stand-out tomato appetizer. Did you know lycopene, the antioxidant found in red tomatoes, is proven to reduce the risk of prostate cancer in men?

MAKES: 16 servings (bread + about 2 tablespoons topping) · **PREP TIME:** 10 minutes · **COOK TIME:** 10 minutes ·

1 loaf French bread

1 1/2 cups finely chopped assorted or red tomatoes (about 1 1/2 pounds, seeded)

1/4 cup chopped onion

1 teaspoon minced garlic

2 teaspoons olive oil

1 teaspoon balsamic vinegar

5–6 fresh basil leaves, chopped or 1 teaspoon dried basil leaves

1 Preheat oven 450°F. Slice French bread into thin slices and bake about 10 minutes or until crispy. Remove from oven.

2 In bowl, combine all remaining ingredients. When ready to serve, top toasted bread with tomato mixture.

TERRIFIC

To seed tomatoes: cut tomato in half from side to side and gently squeeze tomato to watch seeds easily pop out. Canned tomatoes may be used, drain well.

SERVING
SUGGESTION

Make mixture and keep in refrigerator for super snack, pick up, or any time appetizer.

NUTRITIONAL INFORMATION Calories 92, Calories from Fat 11%, Fat 1 g, Saturated Fat 0 g, Cholesterol 0 mg, Sodium 147 mg, Carbohydrates 17 g, Dietary Fiber 1 g, Total Sugars 1 g, Protein 4 g

DIETARY EXCHANGES 1 starch

CANCER

SPINACH ARTICHOKE DIP

What's best about this recipe is it doubles as delicious dip or side—I've served it both ways.
One taste and this was a slam dunk winner boasting flavors of rich, creamy Brie.

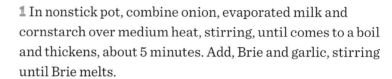

MAKES: 20 (1/4 cup) servings · **PREP TIME:** 15 minutes · **COOK TIME:** About 5–10 minutes ·

1/2 cup chopped onion

1 (12-ounce) can evaporated skimmed milk

2 tablespoons cornstarch

4 ounces Brie cheese, rind removed and cubed

1/2 teaspoon minced garlic

2/3 cup skim milk

2 (10-ounce) packages frozen chopped spinach, thawed and well drained

1 (14-ounce) can quartered artichoke hearts, drained and coarsely chopped

Salt and pepper to taste

1 In nonstick pot, combine onion, evaporated milk and cornstarch over medium heat, stirring, until comes to a boil and thickens, about 5 minutes. Add, Brie and garlic, stirring until Brie melts.

2 Add milk, stirring until heated and bubbly. Stir in spinach and artichokes, heating well. Season to taste.

Skip the chips and try serving with assorted vegetables such as red pepper squares, cucumber, squash, and zucchini rounds. Serve in a hollowed out bread for easy clean up.

I had so many requests for a gluten-free spinach dip so here it is!

NUTRITIONAL INFORMATION Calories 52, Calories from Fat 29%, Fat 2 g, Saturated Fat 1 g, Cholesterol 7 mg, Sodium 119 mg, Carbohydrates 6 g, Dietary Fiber 1 g, Total Sugars 3 g, Protein 4 g
DIETARY EXCHANGES 1/2 other carbohydrate, 1/2 lean meat

GREAT GREEK CHICKEN QUESADILLAS

Mothers know best and when I tested this recipe, my mother said these were the best quesadillas ever.
Garden fresh and simple ingredients for a nutrient-rich last-minute meal or appetizer.

MAKES: 32 (1-quarter quesadilla) servings · **PREP TIME:** 15 minutes · **COOK TIME:** 5 minutes ·

1 cup chopped cooked chicken breast (rotisserie), skin removed

1/2 cup crumbled reduced-fat feta cheese

1/3 cup chopped red onion

1/2 cup chopped peeled cucumber

1/2 cup sliced grape tomatoes

1/4 cup sliced Kalamata olives

1 cup finely chopped fresh baby spinach leaves

1 teaspoon dried oregano leaves

16 (8-inch) flour tortillas

1 In large bowl, combine all ingredients except tortillas.

2 Heat large nonstick skillet coated with nonstick cooking spray and add tortilla. Cover with about 1/2 cup chicken mixture and top with another tortilla.

3 Cook quesadillas, over medium heat 2–4 minutes or until light brown, carefully turning once and pressing down with spatula to melt cheese.

4 Repeat with remaining tortillas and mixture. Cut each quesadilla into fourths.

Keep quesadillas warm on baking sheet in 300°F oven.

To easily cut quesadillas, try using kitchen scissors.

Turn filling into a wrap or makes a great Greek chopped salad.

NUTRITIONAL INFORMATION Calories 75, Calories from Fat 11%, Fat 1 g, Saturated Fat 0 g, Cholesterol 5 mg, Sodium 237 mg, Carbohydrates 13 g, Dietary Fiber 1 g, Total Sugars 0 g, Protein 4 g

DIETARY EXCHANGES 1 starch

CANCER

RED BEAN DIP

Send your taste buds to New Orleans for this classic combination of savory sausage, canned red beans, salsa and seasonings that instantly turns into a spectacular and hearty dip.

MAKES: 24 (1/4-cup) servings · **PREP TIME:** 10 minutes · **COOK TIME:** 20 minutes ·

---

1 cup chopped reduced-fat sausage

2 (15-ounce) cans red kidney beans, rinsed and drained

1 (4-ounce) can chopped green chiles

3/4 cup salsa

1/2 cup nonfat sour cream

1 teaspoon chili powder

1 teaspoon ground cumin

1 1/2 cups shredded reduced-fat Mexican-blend cheese, divided

1 Preheat oven 350°F.

2 Heat nonstick skillet over medium heat, and cook sausage until crisp brown, about 5 minutes. Set aside.

3 In food processor, combine remaining ingredients, reserving 1 cup cheese. Process until mixture is smooth.

4 Transfer to baking dish, sprinkle with remaining cheese, top with sausage. Bake about 15 minutes or until cheese is melted and dip is hot.

Beans are a good source of fiber, which has been shown to reduce the risk of cancer such as colon cancer.

NUTRITIONAL INFORMATION Calories 72, Calories from Fat 23%, Fat 2 g, Saturated Fat 1 g, Cholesterol 7 mg, Sodium 234 mg, Carbohydrates 8 g, Dietary Fiber 2 g, Total Sugars 1 g, Protein 5 g

DIETARY EXCHANGES 1/2 starch, 1/2 lean meat

CORN, CUCUMBER AND TOMATO SALAD

A bullet-proof, fresh and tasty recipe with crunchy cool cucumbers, ripe juicy tomatoes, creamy avocados and corn. An easy nutrition-loaded side dish to any meal.

MAKES: 5 (2/3 cup) servings · **PREP TIME:** 10 minutes · **COOK TIME:** None ·

---

1 cup corn

1 cup peeled chopped cucumber

1 cup chopped tomatoes

1/4 cup chopped red onion

1/4 cup chopped avocado

2 tablespoons lime juice

1 tablespoon nonfat plain
Greek yogurt

1 In large bowl, combine corn, cucumber, tomatoes, onion and avocado.

2 In small bowl, combine lime juice and yogurt. Drizzle over salad. Refrigerate.

SERVING SUGGESTION

Pairs perfectly with grilled or baked fish on a warm summer day.

NUTRITIONAL INFORMATION Calories 53, Calories from Fat 24%, Fat 2 g, Saturated Fat 0 g, Cholesterol 0 mg, Sodium 10 mg, Carbohydrates 10 g, Dietary Fiber 2 g, Total Sugars 4 g, Protein 2 g

DIETARY EXCHANGES 1/2 starch, 1/2 fat

CANCER

SHRIMP PAELLA SALAD

Put the rice on to cook and start prepping the ingredients for this crowd pleasing Spanish style rice entree salad with shrimp, artichokes, tomatoes, peas and prosciutto that's devilishly delicious!

MAKES: 8 (1 1/3-cup) servings · **PREP TIME:** 15 minutes · **COOK TIME:** 20 minutes

2 (5-ounce) packages saffron yellow rice

1/4 cup balsamic vinegar

1/4 cup lemon juice

1 tablespoon olive oil

1 teaspoon dried basil leaves

1 pound medium cooked and peeled shrimp

1 (14-ounce) can quartered artichoke hearts, drained

3/4 cup chopped green bell pepper

1 cup frozen green peas, thawed

1 cup chopped tomato

1/2 cup chopped red onion

2 ounces chopped prosciutto

1 Prepare rice according to package directions; set aside.

2 In small bowl, mix together vinegar, lemon juice, oil and basil; set aside.

3 In large bowl, combine cooked rice with shrimp, artichoke hearts, bell pepper, peas, tomato, red onion, and prosciutto, mixing well.

4 Pour dressing over rice mixture, tossing to coat. Refrigerate until serving.

TERRIFIC TIP

Paella is a Spanish dish of saffron-flavored rice combined with a variety of meats, shellfish, garlic, onions, peas, artichoke hearts, and tomatoes. Chicken may be used for shrimp.

NUTRITION NUGGET

Artichokes are a naturally low-sodium, fat-free, low calorie food, rich in healthy antioxidants and phytonutrients.

NUTRITIONAL INFORMATION Calories 253, Calories from Fat 11%, Fat 3 g, Saturated Fat 1 g, Cholesterol 113 mg, Sodium 762 mg, Carbohydrates 37 g, Dietary Fiber 2 g, Total Sugars 5 g, Protein 21 g
DIETARY EXCHANGES 2 starch, 1 vegetable, 2 1/2 lean meat

CHICKEN SALAD WITH PINEAPPLE VINAIGRETTE

Fast and fabulous, and tastes like a million dollar nutritious salad. I kicked this chicken salad up a notch adding pineapple, healthy leafy kale, and toasty pecans tossed with a subtle, sweet tropical pineapple vinaigrette.

MAKES: 8 (1-cup) servings · PREP TIME: 15 minutes · COOK TIME: None ·

3 cups diced cooked chicken breast (rotisserie), skin removed

1 cup red grapes, cut in half

1 (15-ounce) can pineapple chunks, drained or 2 cups fresh pineapple chunks

1 bunch green onions, chopped

1/3 cup pecan halves, toasted

1/2 cup chopped celery

2 cups chopped kale

PINEAPPLE VINAIGRETTE

2 teaspoons Dijon mustard

Salt and pepper to taste

2 tablespoons olive oil

1/2 cup pineapple juice

1 tablespoon honey

1 In large bowl, combine chicken, grapes, pineapple, green onions, pecans, celery, and kale.

2 *For the Pineapple Vinaigrette:* In small bowl, whisk together all ingredients. Toss with salad.

There is over 100% of your recommended daily amount of Vitamin C in 1 cup of pineapple; acting as an antioxidant and protecting against cancer.

NUTRITIONAL INFORMATION Calories 209, Calories from Fat 36%, Fat 9 g, Saturated Fat 1 g, Cholesterol 47 mg, Sodium 225 mg, Carbohydrates 17 g, Dietary Fiber 3 g, Total Sugars 12 g, Protein 17 g

DIETARY EXCHANGES 1 fruit, 2 1/2 lean meat

CHICKEN AND BROCCOLI STIR-FRY

You can whip up this amazing chicken and broccoli stir-fry quicker than you can pick up take out, not to mention it is so much better for you! Serve over rice.

MAKES: 7 (1-cup) servings · **PREP TIME:** 15 minutes · **COOK TIME:** 15–20 minutes ·

1 1/2 pounds skinless, boneless chicken breasts, cut into thin strips

3 tablespoons cornstarch

3 tablespoons olive oil

4 cups broccoli florets

1 red bell pepper, cored and cut into strips

2 teaspoons minced garlic

3 tablespoons low-sodium soy sauce

1 tablespooon honey

1 1/2 teaspoons finely chopped fresh ginger or 1/2 teaspoon ground ginger

1 In large bowl, toss chicken with cornstarch.

2 In large nonstick skillet, heat olive oil and stir-fry chicken until lightly browned and almost done, about 5–7 minutes.

3 Add broccoli and bell pepper; continue to cook until crisp tender, about 5 minutes.

4 In small bowl, combine garlic, soy sauce, honey and ginger; add to skillet. Cook another few minutes until chicken is thoroughly coated and well heated.

Red peppers too pricey? Just subsitute green bell peppers.

You can store fresh ginger in your freezer to always have on hand.

Did you know that red bell pepper has more vitamin C than an orange?

NUTRITIONAL INFORMATION Calories 213, Calories from Fat 36%, Fat 9 g, Saturated Fat 1 g, Cholesterol 62 mg, Sodium 298 mg, Carbohydrates 11 g, Dietary Fiber 2 g, Total Sugars 5 g, Protein 23 g
DIETARY EXCHANGES 1 vegetable, 1/2 other carbohydrate, 3 lean meat

CAPRESE CHICKEN

Pile on classic fresh Italian ingredients, tomatoes, basil and mozzarella—oven baked
with chicken for a quick trip to Italy. Serve with angel hair pasta.

MAKES: 4 servings · PREP TIME: 10 minutes · COOK TIME: 40–45 minutes ·

3 cups chopped Roma tomatoes

1 cup chopped onion

1 (14-ounce) can artichoke hearts
quartered, drained

1 tablespoon minced garlic

2 tablespoons olive oil

3 tablespoons balsamic vinegar

Salt and pepper to taste

1 1/2 pounds boneless, skinless
thin chicken breasts or tenders

2 ounces fresh mozzarella,
thinly sliced

1/4 cup fresh chopped basil leaves

1 Preheat oven 375°F. In large oblong baking dish, combine
tomatoes, onion, artichoke hearts, garlic, olive oil and
balsamic vinegar. Season to taste.

2 Add chicken breasts and toss with tomato mixture
spreading out in prepared dish. Bake 30–40 minutes or until
chicken is tender.

3 Remove from oven and top chicken breasts with
mozzarella. Return to oven 5 minutes or until cheese is
melted. Sprinkle with basil.

*Lean chicken breasts
are cooked with high
fiber fresh ingredients.*

*If you like more cheese, use extra
slices. Dried basil leaves and
grated part-skim mozzarella
cheese may be substituted for
fresh cheese and basil.*

NUTRITIONAL INFORMATION Calories 384, Calories from Fat 35%, Fat 15 g, Saturated Fat 3 g, Cholesterol 123 mg, Sodium 517 mg,
Carbohydrates 17 g, Dietary Fiber 3 g, Total Sugars 9 g, Protein 45 g
DIETARY EXCHANGES 3 vegetable, 5 lean meat

CANCER

OVEN FRIED FISH

If fried fish is your preferred preparation for fish, you just won the lottery
with this winning fantastic healthy-fried fish recipe.

MAKES: 6 servings · **PREP TIME:** 20 minutes · **COOK TIME:** 20 minutes ·

---

2 tablespoons olive oil

2/3 cup buttermilk

Hot sauce to taste

2 teaspoons Dijon mustard

1 teaspoon minced garlic

Salt and pepper to taste

1 1/2 pounds fish fillets

2/3 cup all-purpose flour

2/3 cup yellow cornmeal

1 Preheat oven 475°F. Coat baking pan with olive oil and put pan in oven to heat.

2 In plastic zip-top resealable bag or glass dish, combine buttermilk, hot sauce, mustard and garlic. Season fish to taste and add fish to buttermilk mixture. Let sit 15 minutes.

3 In shallow bowl or plate, mix flour and cornmeal together. Remove fish from buttermilk, letting excess drip off, and dredge on both sides with cornmeal mixture. Transfer to hot baking pan.

4 Bake 6 minutes, then carefully turn fish and continue baking 5 minutes more, or until cooked through and golden.

The secret trick to crispy fish is to make sure to start with a hot pan.

Don't have buttermilk? Add 1 tablespoon lemon juice or vinegar to 1 cup milk.

Fish like salmon, halibut and tuna is a good source of healthy unsaturated fat.

NUTRITIONAL INFORMATION Calories 173, Calories from Fat 24%, Fat 4 g, Saturated Fat 1 g, Cholesterol 44 mg, Sodium 93 mg, Carbohydrates 13 g, Dietary Fiber 1 g, Total Sugars 1 g, Protein 20 g

DIETARY EXCHANGES 1 starch, 3 lean meat

SALMON AND KALE PASTA

Not sure how to cook these powerhouse foods, kale and salmon? Toss with pasta!
Simple ingredients with easy preparation for an incredibly fresh-flavored salmon dish.

MAKES: 7 (1-cup) servings · **PREP TIME:** 15 minutes · **COOK TIME:** 20 minutes ·

1 pound skinless salmon fillet

Salt and pepper to taste

2 tablespoons lemon juice, divided

8 ounces rotini pasta

2 tablespoons olive oil, divided

3 cups packed fresh baby kale

1 cup chopped tomatoes

1 teaspoon minced garlic

1/4 cup chopped green onions, stems only

Grated Parmesan cheese, optional

1 Preheat oven to 425°F. Cover baking pan with foil and coat with nonstick cooking spray.

2 Season salmon to taste. Drizzle with 1 tablespoon lemon juice. Roast salmon 12 minutes or until flakes with fork. Cut into chunks.

3 Meanwhile, cook pasta according to directions. Drain; set aside.

4 In large nonstick skillet, heat olive oil and quickly cook kale, tomatoes and garlic until kale is slightly wilted, about 3 minutes. Add remaining tablespoon lemon juice.

5 Carefully stir in pasta and salmon, cooking until well heated. Top with green onions and Parmesan cheese, if desired.

You can substitute baby spinach for the kale.

At least two servings of fish (fatty fish preferred) per week for heart health is the recommended intake by the American Heart Association.

NUTRITIONAL INFORMATION Calories 260, Calories from Fat 27%, Fat 8 g, Saturated Fat 1 g, Cholesterol 30 mg, Sodium 66 mg, Carbohydrates 28 g, Dietary Fiber 2 g, Total Sugars 2 g, Protein 19 g

DIETARY EXCHANGES 1 1/2 starch, 1 vegetable, 2 lean meat

CANCER

QUICK LEMON SHRIMP

Prepare my five-ingredient shrimp recipe with lemon, parsley, and garlic and watch your popularity soar. Tryptophan-rich shrimp helps to relax and de-stress you—sometimes that's what you need.

MAKES: 4 servings · PREP TIME: 20 minutes · COOK TIME: 10 minutes ·

1/3 cup chopped parsley

1/4 cup lemon juice

1 teaspoon minced garlic

2 tablespoons olive oil

1 pound peeled medium-large shrimp

Salt and pepper to taste

1 Preheat oven 400°F. Coat shallow baking dish or ramekins with nonstick cooking spray.

2 In bowl, combine parsley, lemon juice and garlic. In another bowl, mix olive oil and shrimp. Season to taste. Transfer shrimp to prepared baking dish.

3 Spread parsley mixture evenly over shrimp. Bake about 8–10 minutes or until shrimp is done.

NUTRITION NUGGET

Shrimp is a great source of protein and takes longer to digest than fats and sugars, making you feel full.

TERRIFIC TIP

I sometimes add crushed red pepper to the parsley mixture for an extra kick!

SERVING SUGGESTION

Serve over Angel Hair Pasta (recipe page 131).

NUTRITIONAL INFORMATION Calories 162, Calories from Fat 40%, Fat 7 g, Saturated Fat 1 g, Cholesterol 183 mg, Sodium 138 mg, Carbohydrates 2 g, Dietary Fiber 0 g, Total Sugars 0 g, Protein 23 g

DIETARY EXCHANGES 3 lean meat

BUTTERNUT SQUASH, BLACK BEAN AND FETA ENCHILADAS

Who says vegetarian meals are boring? Five trendy ingredients have these
nutrient rich enchiladas enticing and exciting the senses!

MAKES: 8 enchiladas · PREP TIME: 15 minutes · COOK TIME: 45 minutes ·

4 cups peeled butternut squash

1 (15-ounce) can black beans, rinsed and drained

1 bunch green onions, chopped

3/4 cup crumbled reduced-fat feta cheese, divided

2 cups salsa verde

8 large (about 7-inch) corn or flour tortillas

1 Preheat oven 400°F. Coat baking pan with foil and coat with nonstick cooking spray.

2 Place squash on prepared pan. Bake 20–25 minutes or until squash is tender but not mushy.

3 Reduce heat to 350°F. In bowl, combine cooked squash, black beans, green onions and 1/2 cup feta.

4 Coat 3-quart oblong baking dish with nonstick cooking spray and spread a little of salsa verde on the bottom. Fill tortillas with about 1/2 cup filling, rolling up and place seam side down in dish. Pour remaining sauce over enchiladas. Sprinkle remaining feta over sauce.

5 Cover pan with foil. Bake 20 minutes or until well heated.

TERRIFIC TIP

Roasted vegetables are easy to prepare with easy clean-up, and roasting really brings out their flavor. Look for pre-cut butternut squash in grocery.

Make this recipe gluten free with corn tortillas.

NUTRITIONAL INFORMATION Calories 202, Calories from Fat 13%, Fat 3 g, Saturated Fat 1 g, Cholesterol 5 mg, Sodium 539 mg, Carbohydrates 36 g, Dietary Fiber 7 g, Total Sugars 7 g, Protein 8 g
DIETARY EXCHANGES 2 starch, 1 vegetable, 1 lean meat

CANCER

WHITE SPINACH AND ARTICHOKE PESTO PIZZA

A pizza with pizazz! Veggies, spinach and artichokes in a light creamy pesto white sauce make this truly a standout vegetarian pizza. Leftover or rotisserie chicken may be added, if you prefer.

MAKES: 8 servings · PREP TIME: 10 minutes · COOK TIME: 10 minutes ·

1 cup skim milk

2 tablespoons all-purpose flour

1 tablespoon basil pesto (jarred)

1 (12-inch) thin pizza crust

1 cup coarsely chopped fresh baby spinach leaves

Half small red onion, thinly sliced and halved

1 (14-ounce) can quartered artichokes, drained

1 cup shredded part-skim mozzarella cheese

1 teaspoon dried basil leaves

1 teaspoon dried oregano leaves

1 Preheat oven 425°F.

2 In small nonstick pot, combine milk and flour over medium heat, stirring until thickened. Remove from heat and add pesto.

3 Spread over crust. Top with spinach, onion and artichokes. Sprinkle with mozzarella cheese, basil, and oregano.

4 Bake 10 minutes or until crust is golden brown and cheese is melted.

Instead of picking up a frozen pizza, make your own for the freezer. Don't cook before freezing.

NUTRITION NUGGET

Spinach is chock-full of nutrition, as evidenced by its vibrant rich green color—concentrated in phytonutrients and flavonoids, offering healthy antioxidant protection.

NUTRITIONAL INFORMATION Calories 171, Calories from Fat 27%, Fat 5 g, Saturated Fat 2 g, Cholesterol 10 mg, Sodium 395 mg, Carbohydrates 21 g, Dietary Fiber 1 g, Total Sugars 3 g, Protein 10 g
DIETARY EXCHANGES 1 starch, 1 vegetable, 1 lean meat

ROASTED CAULIFLOWER

Cruciferous cauliflower gets a magical makeover with a few southwestern seasonings and a touch of lime.

MAKES: 6 (1/2- cup) servings · **PREP TIME:** 5 minutes · **COOK TIME:** 30 minutes ·

1/4 cup lime juice

1 tablespoon olive oil

2 teaspoons chili powder

1 teaspoon ground cumin

1/2 teaspoon garlic powder

1 medium head cauliflower, cut into florets (about 4 cups)

1 Preheat oven 400°F. Line baking pan with foil and coat with nonstick cooking spray.

2 In small bowl, whisk together lime juice, olive oil, chili powder, cumin and garlic powder. Toss with cauliflower florets until well coated.

3 Bake 25–30 minutes, stirring occasionally, until cauliflower is tender.

Look for pre-washed and bagged cauliflower for extra ease.

NUTRITIONAL INFORMATION Calories 45, Calories from Fat 47%, Fat 3 g, Saturated Fat 0 g, Cholesterol 0 mg, Sodium 37 mg, Carbohydrates 5 g, Dietary Fiber 2 g, Total Sugars 2 g, Protein 2 g

DIETARY EXCHANGES 1 vegetable, 1/2 fat

CANCER

BRUSSELS SPROUTS STIR-FRY

Fresh Brussels sprouts are so much more delicious than what we thought as kids!
Time to give this unassuming vegetable a chance—I promise you won't be disappointed!

MAKES: 4 servings · PREP TIME: 10 minutes · COOK TIME: 15 minutes ·

1 pound Brussels sprouts

3 tablespoons olive oil, divided

1/2 cup chopped onion

Salt and pepper to taste

Crushed red pepper flakes

1 Cut ends off Brussels sprouts and slice in half.

2 In medium nonstick skillet coated with nonstick cooking spray, heat 1 tablespoon olive oil, and sauté onion about 5 minutes or until tender. Remove from pan.

3 In same pan coated with nonstick cooking spray, heat remaining 2 tablespoons olive oil, and place Brussels sprout halves face down in skillet until golden brown, around 5 minutes.

4 Return onion to skillet, and cook about 10 minutes, stirring occasionally, until Brussels sprouts are tender. Season to taste.

NUTRITION NUGGET

Brussels sprouts provide awesome DNA protective and cancer preventative benefits so keep them on your weekly menu.

NUTRITIONAL INFORMATION Calories 146, Calories from Fat 60%, Fat 10 g, Saturated Fat 1 g, Cholesterol 0 mg, Sodium 29 mg, Carbohydrates 12 g, Dietary Fiber 5 g, Total Sugars 3 g, Protein 4 g

DIETARY EXCHANGES 2 vegetable, 2 fat

GERD

GERD
WHY DOES MY HEART BURN?

WHAT IS GERD?
WHAT CAUSES GERD?
HOW DO I GET GERD UNDER CONTROL?

Anytime the stomach is stretched, no matter what food is put into it, acid gets produced by special cells in the stomach lining; the acid is used to help digest food. Pyrosis, or "heartburn" is that burning, gnawing feeling in the stomach that typically occurs between 30–60 minutes after a meal, any meal.

The acid that is produced by the stomach is supposed to stay in the stomach, and then move downstream into the small intestine—the next compartment in the food digestion process. However, in certain men, the acid mixture leaks backwards through a valve and back into the esophagus—the swallowing tube that leads from the mouth to the stomach.

While the lining of the stomach is perfectly suited to handle acid, the esophagus is not. And when the lining of the esophagus gets exposed to stomach acid, it becomes injured and inflamed (esophagitis). This acid sensation feels like a burn. To make matters worse, the esophagus is anatomically located right behind the heart, so when this happens—it literally can feel like your "heart is burning," thus the term "heartburn."

The more the esophagus is exposed to acid, the more damaged the esophageal valve becomes, which leads to more leaking of acid. Chronic acid irritation of the esophagus can lead to a pre-cancerous condition called Barrett's Esophagus

Heartburn from this mechanism is called Gastroesophageal Reflux disease, or GERD for short. GERD is responsible for millions of dollars in medical costs from expensive medications and also from many unnecessary trips to the emergency room for "chest pain" which turns out to be simply GERD.

Conditions That Lead to GERD:

* *Obesity*—the fat in the belly literally weighs on the stomach, which forces food backwards
* *Smoking*—weakens the esophageal valve
* *Hiatal Hernia*—bulge of the stomach up through the diaphragm and into the chest
* *Diabetes*—damages the nerves that normally empty the stomach

Treatment of GERD:

* *Weight loss*—maintain a healthy diet, and try eating smaller meals
* *Stop smoking*
* *Don't lie down after a meal*—wait at least 3 hours after a meal before lying down.
* *Elevate the head of your bed*—Allow gravity to help move things in the right direction
* *Antacids*—neutralize the acid, but don't fix the problem
* *Acid blocking or inhibiting medications*—typically need to take for a prolonged period to allow esophageal sphincter valve time to heal.

The GERD Diet

GERD is an extremely painful condition that should be prevented through diet whenever possible. Because it can be different for each individual, a food diary can be helpful to identify your personal food triggers that cause or worsen your GERD symptoms. Certain foods are common GERD culprits and should be avoided.

Small meals can be a good solution to reduce the risk of stomach acid leaking back up the esophagus, and avoid eating a large meal before bed. Never lie down immediately after eating.

Weight loss is often a successful step in reducing GERD because belly fat worsens reflux symptoms. Hand in hand with obesity, diabetes can also be an underlying cause of GERD. By choosing trim and terrific, high fiber, unprocessed whole foods, lean meat, fruits and vegetables, you will start reducing your weight and in turn reducing your risk for GERD.

Diet and lifestyle changes often begin with what to avoid. These include things that can trigger or worsen symptoms.

Common High Risk Foods for GERD:

- High fat foods (fried foods, whole milk, cream soups, oils, fast food)
- Caffeine
- Chocolate
- Onions
- Peppermint or spearmint
- Citrus
- Tomato products
- Spicy foods
- Carbonated beverages
- Alcohol
- Nicotine

Sweet Potato Biscuits **PAGE 137** with Honey Mustard Pork **PAGE 136**

OVERNIGHT OATMEAL

Forget picking up breakfast when you can have this fiber full oatmeal for the perfect healthy breakfast on-the-go. Make it your own with your favorite toppings.

MAKES: 1 (1 1/2 cups) serving · PREP TIME: 5 minutes · COOK TIME: Overnight refrigeration ·

3/4 cup old-fashioned oatmeal

3/4 cup orange juice

2 tablespoons skim milk

1 In mason jar or container with lid, the night before mix together all ingredients.

2 Next morning top with toppings of your choice.

 Mix in a scoop of your favorite protein powder for added satiety and to help level blood sugar.

SERVING SUGGESTION *Favorite nutritious toppings include coconut, walnuts, fresh fruit, and cinnamon—add brown sugar, maple syrup or honey for a sweeter oatmeal.*

NUTRITIONAL INFORMATION Calories 319, Calories from Fat 13%, Fat 5 g, Saturated Fat 1 g, Cholesterol 1 mg, Sodium 15 mg, Carbohydrates 60 g, Dietary Fiber 6 g, Total Sugars 19 g, Protein 10 g

DIETARY EXCHANGES 3 starch, 1 fruit

HARD BOILED EGGS

A fail proof method to insure you get perfect hard boiled eggs to eat or toss in recipes.

PREP TIME: None · COOK TIME: 9–12 minutes ·

Eggs

TERRIFIC TIP

This recipe can be used to make as many eggs as you want, depending on the size of the pot you use.

NUTRITION NUGGET

Known as the gold standard for protein quality and content, an egg contains all 9 essential amino acids, along with 9 other amino acids.

1 Place eggs in a single layer in pot, cover with cold water, bring water to boil.

2 Once water comes to hard boil, turn heat off, cover pan, and remove from heat.

3 Allow eggs to sit in water until cooked; about 9 minutes for medium eggs and 12 minutes for large eggs.

4 When timer goes off, remove eggs from pan and transfer to large bowl of cool water. When eggs reach room temperature, peel eggs.

NUTRITIONAL INFORMATION Calories 71, Calories from Fat 62%, Fat 5 g, Saturated Fat 2 g, Cholesterol 186 mg, Sodium 71 mg, Carbohydrates 0 g, Dietary Fiber 0 g, Total Sugars 0 g, Protein 6 g

DIETARY EXCHANGES 1 lean meat

BANANA BLUEBERRY BREAD

Never made a quick bread? With a bowl, a spoon, Bisquick mix, blueberries, and bananas,
you can whip up this fruity, moist bread for a wonderful breakfast or snack.

MAKES: 16 slices · **PREP TIME:** 10 minutes · **COOK TIME:** 40–45 minutes ·

---

1 2/3 cups mashed bananas

2/3 cup light brown sugar

2 eggs

1 3/4 cups biscuit baking mix

1 teaspoon ground cinnamon

1 cup chopped pecans or walnuts, optional

1 cup blueberries

1 Preheat oven 350°F. Coat 9×5×3-inch loaf pan with nonstick cooking spray.

2 In large mixing bowl, mix bananas, brown sugar and eggs. Stir in biscuit mix, cinnamon and nuts, if using, until just blended. Carefully stir in blueberries and transfer to prepared pan.

3 Bake 40–45 minutes or until toothpick inserted in center comes out clean.

Over-ripe bananas? Freeze—with or without peels—in plastic freezer zip-top bags for your next batch of banana bread.

Bananas are a great source of potassium and are easily digested by virtually everyone.

NUTRITIONAL INFORMATION Calories 124, Calories from Fat 17%, Fat 2 g, Saturated Fat 1 g, Cholesterol 23 mg, Sodium 174 mg, Carbohydrates 25 g, Dietary Fiber 1 g, Total Sugars 13 g, Protein 2 g

DIETARY EXCHANGES 1 1/2 starch

POTATO SOUP

How could this creamy, comforting potato soup be so simple and so delicious?
Start with hash browns (no potato peeling) and top with desired condiments.

MAKES: 8 (1-cup) servings · **PREP TIME:** 5 minutes · **COOK TIME:** 20 minutes ·

---

6 cups frozen hash brown
    potatoes, partially thawed

6 cups reduced-sodium fat-free
    vegetable or chicken broth

1 cup chopped onion, optional

1/4 cup all-purpose flour

1 (12-ounce) can evaporated
    skimmed milk, divided

3/4 cup nonfat plain Greek yogurt

Salt and pepper to taste

Optional toppings: Green onions,
    cheese, turkey bacon

1 In large nonstick pot, combine hash browns, broth, and onion, if desired; bring to boil, reduce heat, and cook, covered, 8–10 minutes.

2 In small bowl, whisk together flour with 1/3 cup evaporated milk. Add to potato mixture with remaining milk. Bring to boil, reduce heat, and cook, stirring, 5 minutes or until thickened.

3 Remove from heat and stir in yogurt; don't boil after adding, stirring until well combined. Season to taste.

4 Top with green onions, cheese, and chopped turkey bacon when serving, if desired.

This diabetes-friendly potato soup recipe is low-sodium only if you use reduced-sodium broth.

NUTRITION NUGGET

I like using Greek yogurt as it is richer and creamier than plain yogurt, while being protein-rich and low in sugar.

NUTRITIONAL INFORMATION Calories 195, Calories from Fat 0%, Fat 0 g, Saturated Fat 0 g, Cholesterol 2 mg, Sodium 137 mg, Carbohydrates 38 g, Dietary Fiber 3 g, Total Sugars 7 g, Protein 10 g
DIETARY EXCHANGES 2 starch, 1/2 fat-free milk

ANGEL HAIR PASTA

This simple and tasty pasta with a few added ingredients pops with flavor and goes great with any meal, giving you lots of bang for your buck!

MAKES: 9 (2/3-cup) servings · PREP TIME: 5 minutes · COOK TIME: 15 minutes ·

1 (12-ounce) package angel hair pasta

3 tablespoons olive oil

1/2 teaspoon minced garlic

1 tablespoon finely chopped parsley

1 Cook pasta according to directions on package. Drain and set aside.

2 In small skillet, combine all remaining ingredients and sauté a few minutes. Pour over cooked pasta and toss. Serve immediately.

When a smaller amount of parsley is called for, dried parsley works fine.

Keep a jar of minced garlic in the refrigerator for a short cut.

Use as a side or makes great light meal.

NUTRITIONAL INFORMATION Calories 180, Calories from Fat 26%, Fat 5 g, Saturated Fat 1 g, Cholesterol 0 mg, Sodium 3 mg, Carbohydrates 28 g, Dietary Fiber 1 g, Total Sugars 1 g, Protein 5 g

DIETARY EXCHANGES 2 starch, 1/2 fat

BEST BAKED CHICKEN

Only five pantry-friendly ingredients turn lean chicken breast tenders into your next speedy chicken and gravy favorite dinner.

MAKES: 4 servings · PREP TIME: 10 minutes · COOK TIME: 60–70 minutes ·

1 1/2 pounds chicken breasts or tenders
1/4 cup biscuit baking mix
1 tablespoon olive oil
1 teaspoon minced garlic
1 tablespoon all-purpose flour
1 (16-ounce) can low-sodium fat-free chicken broth

1 Preheat oven 375°F. Coat 3-quart oblong baking dish with nonstick cooking spray.

2 Coat chicken in baking mix and place in prepared dish. Bake 40 minutes.

3 In small nonstick pot, combine oil and garlic; add flour. Whisk in chicken broth, bring to boil, and cook until slightly thickened.

4 Pour over chicken, cover with foil, and continue baking another 20–30 minutes, or until chicken is done.

Lean protein choices such as chicken breast along with a diet full of unprocessed whole foods help keep your weight within a healthy range which in turn lessens painful GERD symptoms.

Serve with rice to soak up the last drop of gravy.

NUTRITIONAL INFORMATION Calories 259, Calories from Fat 30%, Fat 9 g, Saturated Fat 2 g, Cholesterol 109 mg, Sodium 295 mg, Carbohydrates 5 g, Dietary Fiber 0 g, Total Sugars 0 g, Protein 38 g
DIETARY EXCHANGES 1/2 starch, 5 lean meat

OVEN CHICKEN RISOTTO

Don't get intimidated with risotto. For my easy recipe, toss the ingredients into a baking dish and pop in the oven for a tasty chicken dinner. Arborio rice is the type of rice typically used to make risotto.

MAKES: 5 (1-cup) servings · **PREP TIME:** 10 minutes · **COOK TIME:** 35 minutes ·

1 tablespoon olive oil

1/2 pound sliced mushrooms

1 cup Arborio rice

3 cups fat-free chicken broth, divided

2 cups fresh baby spinach leaves

2 cups coarsely chopped cooked chicken breasts (rotisserie), skin removed

1/3 cup grated Parmesan cheese, optional

Salt and pepper to taste

1 Preheat oven 400°F.

2 In small nonstick skillet, heat oil and sauté mushrooms until tender.

3 In 2-quart oblong baking dish, combine mushrooms, Arborio rice and 2 1/2 cups broth. Bake, covered with foil, 35 minutes or until liquid absorbed.

4 Remove from oven and add 1/2 cup remaining broth and spinach, stirring until rice gets creamy and spinach wilted. Toss in chicken and Parmesan cheese, if desired. Season to taste.

TERRIFIC TIP

Add more broth if needed, to make creamy. Use this basic risotto recipe and add your favorite ingredients.

NUTRITION NUGGET

The only reason this is not a diabetic-friendly recipe is the sodium is a little high.

NUTRITIONAL INFORMATION Calories 268, Calories from Fat 24%, Fat 7 g, Saturated Fat 1 g, Cholesterol 62 mg, Sodium 761 mg, Carbohydrates 31 g, Dietary Fiber 2 g, Total Sugars 1 g, Protein 20 g

DIETARY EXCHANGES 2 starch, 2 lean meat

GERD

CHICKEN AND DUMPLINGS

Nothing beats classic comfort food. With rotisserie chicken, canned broth and drop dumplings—everyone requests this effortless one-dish meal.

MAKES: 8 (1-cup) servings · **PREP TIME:** 10 minutes · **COOK TIME:** 30 minutes ·

1 small onion, chopped, optional

1 1/2 cups baby carrots

1/2 teaspoon minced garlic

1/4 cup all-purpose flour

6 cups fat-free chicken broth, divided

1/2 teaspoon dried thyme leaves

2 cups chopped cooked chicken breast (rotisserie), skin removed

2 cups biscuit baking mix

2/3 cup skim milk

Salt and pepper to taste

1. In large nonstick pot coated with nonstick cooking spray, sauté onion, if desired, carrots, and garlic over medium heat until tender.

2. In small cup, stir flour and 1/3 cup chicken broth, mixing until smooth. Gradually add flour mixture and remaining broth to pot; bring to boil. Add thyme and chicken.

3. In bowl, stir together biscuit baking mix and milk. Drop the mixture by spoonfuls into boiling broth.

4. Return to boil, reduce heat, and cook, covered, carefully stirring occasionally, 15–20 minutes or until dumplings are done. Season to taste. If soup is too thick, add more chicken broth.

A short-cut for dumplings: cut flaky biscuits into fourths and drop into boiling broth.

Use reduced-sodium broth to make this recipe diabetic-friendly. Leave out the onion to make it GERD–friendly.

NUTRITIONAL INFORMATION Calories 218, Calories from Fat 23%, Fat 6 g, Saturated Fat 1 g, Cholesterol 32 mg, Sodium 1207 mg, Carbohydrates 28 g, Dietary Fiber 2 g, Total Sugars 4 g, Protein 15 g
DIETARY EXCHANGES 1 1/2 starch, 1 vegetable, 1 1/2 lean meat

GREEK CHICKEN BURGERS

Craving burgers? Get out of your comfort zone and try this amazing chicken burger with Greek flair.
Serve with sliced red onion, tomato and cucumber, as tolerated.

MAKES: 4 burgers · **PREP TIME:** 10 minutes · **COOK TIME:** 15 minutes ·

---

1 pound ground chicken

1 egg white

1/3 cup bread crumbs

1 teaspoon minced garlic

2 teaspoons dried oregano leaves

1/2 cup coarsely chopped fresh
baby spinach leaves

1/4 cup crumbled reduced-fat
feta cheese

Salt and pepper to taste

1 Preheat oven 500°F. Line baking pan with foil.

2 In large bowl, combine all ingredients and form into four patties. Place on prepared pan and cook 15 minutes or until done.

*Make ahead and freeze
uncooked burgers to pull out
on busy nights. For sliders,
make 12 miniature patties.*

*Get protein into your diet
to help build muscle.*

NUTRITIONAL INFORMATION Calories 192, Calories from Fat 22%, Fat 5 g, Saturated Fat 2 g, Cholesterol 75 mg, Sodium 333 mg, Carbohydrates 8 g, Dietary Fiber 1 g, Total Sugars 1 g, Protein 28 g
DIETARY EXCHANGES 1/2 starch, 3 lean meat

GERD

HONEY MUSTARD PORK TENDERLOIN

Pork tenderloins make a great last minute meal. You can take it to the bank that everyone will request this easy pork tenderloin with a subtly sweet, herby flavor.

MAKES: 6–8 servings · **PREP TIME:** 5 minutes · **COOK TIME:** 40–45 minutes ·

2 tablespoons Dijon mustard

1/2 teaspoon minced garlic

1/2 teaspoon dried rosemary leaves

1/2 teaspoon dried thyme leaves

1/4 teaspoon pepper

2 tablespoons honey

2 (1-pound) pork tenderloins, trimmed of fat

1 Preheat oven 350°F. Line baking pan with foil and coat with nonstick cooking spray.

2 In small bowl, mix together mustard, garlic, rosemary, thyme, pepper, and honey. Coat tenderloins with mixture.

3 Place tenderloins on prepared pan. Bake 40–45 minutes, or until meat thermometer inserted into thickest portion registers 160°F.

Tenderloins come two to a package. If one will be enough for you to serve, halve recipe, and freeze other tenderloin.

Don't have rosemary? Add extra thyme or just leave it out.

Select meat ending in "loin" or "round" for the leanest cuts.

NUTRITIONAL INFORMATION Calories 145, Calories from Fat 18%, Fat 3 g, Saturated Fat 1 g, Cholesterol 74 mg, Sodium 137 mg, Carbohydrates 5 g, Dietary Fiber 0 g, Total Sugars 5 g, Protein 24 g
DIETARY EXCHANGES 1/2 other carbohydrate, 3 lean meat

SWEET POTATO BISCUITS

Breakfast, snack or dinner—these easy, no fuss biscuits made with baking mix are the "real deal."

MAKES: 18 biscuits · **PREP TIME:** 15 minutes · **COOK TIME:** 10–12 minutes ·

4 cups all-purpose baking mix

1/2 teaspoon ground cinnamon

1 (15-ounce) can sweet potatoes, drained, reserve 1/2 cup juice

1/2 cup skim milk

1 Preheat oven 450°F. Coat baking pan with nonstick cooking spray.

2 In large bowl, combine baking mix and cinnamon. Mash sweet potatoes and add to dry mixture with milk and reserved juice, mixing well.

3 Roll on floured surface or press with hands until 1-inch thick. Cut with 2-inch cutter or glass, place on baking pan. Bake 10–12 minutes or until golden.

An incredibly easy dough to work with and may be pressed out with your hands if you don't have a rolling pin.

Use leftover Honey Mustard Pork Tenderloin (page 136) and make pork biscuit sandwiches.

NUTRITIONAL INFORMATION Calories 128, Calories from Fat 24%, Fat 3 g, Saturated Fat 1 g, Cholesterol 0 mg, Sodium 337 mg, Carbohydrates 22 g, Dietary Fiber 1 g, Total Sugars 4 g, Protein 2 g

DIETARY EXCHANGES 1 1/2 starch

PESTO POTATOES

Probably the easiest and best potato dish ever. Three-ingredient amazing crispy
oven roasted potatoes tossed with pesto and Parmesan cheese.

MAKES: 6 (1-cup) servings · PREP TIME: 10 minutes · COOK TIME: 25–35 minutes ·

2 pounds red potatoes, quartered

2 tablespoons basil pesto (jarred)

Salt and pepper to taste

3 tablespoons grated Parmesan
cheese

1 Preheat oven 400°F. Line baking pan with foil and coat with
nonstick cooking spray.

2 In large bowl, toss potatoes and pesto. Transfer potatoes to
prepared pan. Season to taste.

3 Roast 25–35 minutes (depending on size) or until crisp
tender. Sprinkle with Parmesan cheese evenly over the
potatoes. Continue roasting another 3–5 minutes or until
cheese is melted.

⟩NUTRITION⟨ NUGGET

*Certain foods are common GERD
culprits and should be avoided;
but it can be different for each
individual. A food diary can be
helpful to identify your personal
food triggers that cause or worsen
your GERD symptoms.*

TERRIFIC TIP

*Use your basil pesto for the
Pesto Shrimp (page 150) and
White Spinach and Artichoke
Pesto Pizza (page 122).*

NUTRITIONAL INFORMATION Calories 143, Calories from Fat 22%, Fat 4 g, Saturated Fat 1 g, Cholesterol 3 mg, Sodium 110 mg,
Carbohydrates 24 g, Dietary Fiber 3 g, Total Sugars 2 g, Protein 4 g
DIETARY EXCHANGES 1 1/2 starch, 1/2 fat

FIX IT FAST OR
FIX IT SLOW

FIX IT FAST OR FIX IT SLOW
QUICK FIX MEALS & CROCK POT COOKING

What's for dinner? That always seems to be the question. Maybe you have the main dish and you're looking for an easy side dish to round out your meal.

Or, sometimes you just want a quick healthy appetizer or dessert, or meal you can put on the table fast! Everybody needs a few go-to dinner recipes in their back pocket and these are the ingredients you want to keep stocked in your pantry so you know you can throw dinner together at a moment's notice. Whether you are trying to impress or just want to complete a meal, these are my favorite go-to recipes that add fast flavor and are sure to satisfy.

Pantry List of Quick Fixes and Short Cuts:
* Bisquick
* Cake mix
* Cream cheese (reduced-fat)
* Crescent rolls (reduced-fat)
* Frozen hash browns
* Frozen protein—chicken, beef, pork, shrimp, fish
* Frozen vegetables
* Garlic, minced in jar
* Microwave ready brown rice and quinoa
* Rotissiere chicken
* Salsa
* Shredded cheese (reduced-fat)
* Tomato products (canned), Marinara Sauce

Crock Pot Convenience

After much demand through the years for crock pot recipes, I asked my awesome "Facebook friends" what they thought—and WOW, did I get a response! I quickly received over 100 responses saying how much they wanted slow cooker recipes. I have to admit, I was skeptical at first but after trying my hand at crock pot cooking—boy, do I get it now! Slow cookers are the ultimate in convenient cooking, enabling you to cook on your own schedule. What could be better at the end of a long hard day, than a healthy and delicious home-cooked meal that practically cooked itself!

Slow Cooker Tips:
* Check that your cooker is the right size for the recipe you are making.
* Make sure your cooker is at least half full but no more than two-thirds full so foods cook safely in the given time range.
* Look for make-ahead steps. Save valuable morning time by browning the meat or chopping the vegetables the night before.
* Cut slow-cooking vegetables (carrots, potatoes) into small pieces.
* Cut quick-cooking vegetables (squash, bell peppers) into larger pieces.
* Cooking in a slow cooker is great for cooking lean, less-tender cuts of meat. After cooking several hours in liquid, lean meats become moist and tender.
* Save time by skipping browning. Browning adds color and flavor, but you usually can skip this step, if needed.
* Boost flavor by when you add the herbs. Add dried herbs to the slow cooker at the beginning of the cooking; fresh herbs should be added at the end.
* Use slow cooker liners befores adding the ingredients—keeps the clean-up a breeze!

To Stir or Not to Stir

Don't be tempted to lift the lid! When you lift the lid to stir or add ingredients, replace it as quickly as possible, especially when using the LOW setting. An uncovered cooker can lose up to 20° cooking heat in as little as 2 minutes.

BURGER DIP

Forever, this has been my most requested "men's dip." Watching sporting events on TV?
Just four ingredients and 5 minutes for this best, bulletproof dip.

MAKES: 20 (1/4-cup) servings · **PREP TIME:** 5 minutes · **COOK TIME:** 10 minutes ·

---

1 pound ground sirloin

1/2 pound sliced mushrooms

1 (16-ounce) jar salsa

1 (8-ounce) package shredded reduced-fat Mexican-blend cheese

1 In nonstick pot, cook meat and mushrooms over medium heat 5–7 minutes, until meat is done. Drain any excess fat.

2 Add salsa and cheese, stirring over medium heat, until cheese is melted.

Turn leftover dip into a delicious meal tossed with pasta or served over rice.

NUTRITION NUGGET

Research shows that eating high quality protein such as lean beef can support weight loss with appetite control and satiety.

NUTRITIONAL INFORMATION Calories 80, Calories from Fat 50%, Fat 4 g, Saturated Fat 2 g, Cholesterol 23 mg, Sodium 184 mg, Carbohydrates 2 g, Dietary Fiber 0 g, Total Sugars 1 g, Protein 8 g

DIETARY EXCHANGES 1 lean meat

FIX IT FAST OR FIX IT SLOW

QUESO DIP

Craving queso and margaritas? Whip up this gluten-free queso in the time it takes you to make a margarita.

MAKES: 12 (1/4-cup) servings · PREP TIME: 5 minutes · COOK TIME: 5–7 minutes · F ✓ G

1 (12-ounce) can evaporated skim milk

1 tablespoon cornstarch

2 tablespoons reduced-fat cream cheese

1 cup shredded reduced-fat sharp Cheddar cheese

1 (10-ounce) can diced tomatoes and green chilies, drained

1 teaspoon chili powder

1 In large nonstick pot coated with nonstick cooking spray, combine evaporated milk and cornstarch. Bring to boil, stirring constantly, until thickens about 4 minutes.

2 Add remaining ingredients, cooking until cheese is melted and mixture creamy.

Liven up your queso with chopped spinach, ground meat, chicken or whatever sounds good to you!

Serve dip heated with tortilla chips or vegetable rounds.

NUTRITIONAL INFORMATION Calories 64, Calories from Fat 32%, Fat 2 g, Saturated Fat 2 g, Cholesterol 8 mg, Sodium 205 mg, Carbohydrates 5 g, Dietary Fiber 0 g, Total Sugars 4 g, Protein 6 g

DIETARY EXCHANGES 1/2 fat-free milk

BARBECUED SALAMI

Highly requested simple, stand-up kind of appetizer everyone gravitates to.

MAKES: 32 (1-ounce) servings · **PREP TIME:** 5 minutes · **COOK TIME:** 1 hour ·

---

1 2-pound salami (all beef)

1 (16-ounce) jar chunky apricot preserves

1/3 cup Dijon mustard

1 Preheat oven 325°F. Coat baking pan with foil.

2 Remove wrappings from salami. Score diagonally with knife in both directions creating diamond cut and place salami on prepared pan.

3 In small bowl, mix together preserves and mustard. Spoon sauce over and inside salami cuts. Bake about 1 hour or until salami is crisp, spooning sauce on top salami halfway through cooking.

Serve on a cheese tray with toothpicks and Dijon mustard or slices of bread.

NUTRITIONAL INFORMATION Calories 145, Calories from Fat 57%, Fat 9 g, Saturated Fat 3 g, Cholesterol 31 mg, Sodium 521 mg, Carbohydrates 10 g, Dietary Fiber 0 g, Total Sugars 9 g, Protein 6 g

DIETARY EXCHANGES 1/2 other carbohydrates, 1 lean meat, 1 fat

CRAWFISH GUMBO NACHOS

Need some junk food? Give your favorite snack food the most magical cajun makeover with this combination of Louisiana crawfish and savory gumbo ingredients.

MAKES: 16 (1/3 cup chips + little less than 1/4 cup filling) · **PREP TIME:** 10 minutes · **COOK TIME:** 20 minutes

1/2 pound chicken sausage, thinly sliced and halved

1/2 green or red bell pepper, chopped

1 cup chopped onion

2 cups sliced fresh okra

1 teaspoon minced garlic

6 cups oven baked tortilla chips

1 cup Louisiana crawfish tails, rinsed and drained

2 cups shredded reduced-fat Mexican-blend cheese

1 Preheat oven to 400°F. Line baking pan with foil.

2 In large nonstick skillet, cook sausage over medium heat, stirring, until browned, about 5 minutes. Add bell pepper and onion, cooking until tender, about 5 minutes. Add okra and garlic and continue cooking, stirring, about 3–4 minutes.

3 Arrange chips on prepared pan. Spoon okra mixture on top of chips. Top with crawfish and sprinkle with cheese.

4 Bake about 3–4 minutes or until cheese is melted.

TERRIFIC

Make sure you always use Louisiana crawfish. If not in season, keep Louisiana crawfish in your freezer to whip up recipes like this.

Any protein may be substituted.

NUTRITIONAL INFORMATION Calories 126, Calories from Fat 40%, Fat 6 g, Saturated Fat 2 g, Cholesterol 32 mg, Sodium 285 mg, Carbohydrates 11 g, Dietary Fiber 1 g, Total Sugars 1 g, Protein 9 g
DIETARY EXCHANGES 1/2 starch, 1 lean meat, 1/2 fat

SPEEDY SHRIMP AND CORN SOUP

Volunteer to bring soup as you can knock out this super simple, delicious
tomato-based shrimp and corn soup by just opening a few cans.

MAKES: 12 (1-cup) servings · **PREP TIME:** 5 minutes · **COOK TIME:** 10 minutes ·

---

2 (15 1/2-ounce) cans cream-style corn

2 cups frozen corn

2 (14 1/2-ounce) cans diced tomatoes
and green chilies

1 (15-ounce) can tomato sauce

2 pounds medium peeled shrimp

1 bunch green onions, chopped

1 In large nonstick pot, combine cream-style corn, corn,
tomatoes and green chilies and tomato sauce until heated.

2 Add shrimp, bring to boil. Lower heat, cook until shrimp is
done, 5–7 minutes. Sprinkle with green onions.

*This soup can be made
with Louisiana crawfish or
crab instead of shrimp or
leave out seafood for great
vegetarian corn soup.*

*Easily reduce the sodium
by using no-salt cream
style corn to make the
recipe diabetic.*

NUTRITIONAL INFORMATION Calories 169, Calories from Fat 6%, Fat 1 g, Saturated Fat 0 g, Cholesterol 122 mg, Sodium 786 mg,
Carbohydrates 24 g, Dietary Fiber 3 g, Total Sugars 6 g, Protein 18 g
DIETARY EXCHANGES 1 1/2 starch, 1 vegetable, 2 lean meat

CRAWFISH KING CAKE

A recipe with fireworks—this simple, savory king cake is beyond good! Starts with crescent rolls with a scrumptious creamy Louisiana crawfish filling, topped with Mardi Gras colored Parmesan cheese.

MAKES: 14 servings · **PREP TIME:** 20 minutes · **COOK TIME:** 20–25 minutes ·

1/2 cup chopped onion

1/2 cup chopped red or green bell pepper

1 teaspoon minced garlic

1 cup Louisiana crawfish tails, drained and rinsed

1/3 cup chopped green onions

3 tablespoons reduced-fat cream cheese

2 (8-ounce) cans reduced-fat crescent rolls

MARDI GRAS TOPPING

6 tablespoons grated Parmesan cheese

Yellow, green, red, and blue food coloring

1 Preheat oven 350°F. Coat 10-inch round pizza pan lined with foil with nonstick cooking spray.

2 In nonstick skillet coated with nonstick cooking spray, sauté onion, bell pepper and garlic until tender. Add crawfish, green onions and cream cheese, stirring until creamy. Remove from heat.

3 Separate crescent rolls at perforations, into 16 pieces. Place pieces around prepared pan with points in the center. About halfway down from points, press seams together.

4 Spread crawfish mixture on dough in the center where seams are pressed together. Fold dough points over filling, then fold bottom of triangle over points forming circular roll like king cake. Bake about 20–25 minutes or until golden brown.

5 *To make Mardi Gras Topping:* In three small bowls, divide cheese. To each bowl add a few drops of food coloring to color cheese: yellow, green, and purple (blue and red). Sprinkle cheese over baked king cake. Return to oven 1–2 minutes or until cheese is melted.

Think of this as a crawfish bread and make year round with different colored cheese or just use plain cheese.

NUTRITIONAL INFORMATION Calories 134, Calories from Fat 42%, Fat 7 g, Saturated Fat 3 g, Cholesterol 17 mg, Sodium 311 mg, Carbohydrates 15 g, Dietary Fiber 0 g, Total Sugars 3 g, Protein 5 g

DIETARY EXCHANGES 1 starch, 1 fat

CHICKEN TAMALE PIE

Close your eyes and you'll think you're eating the BEST tamales ever!
No worries, you won't believe how easy this recipe is—an ideal quick dinner!

MAKES: 8 servings · **PREP TIME:** 15 minutes · **COOK TIME:** 35–40 minutes ·

1/3 cup skim milk

1 egg

2 tablespoons taco seasoning, divided

1 (14 3/4-ounce) can no-salt cream-style corn

1 (8.5-ounce) box corn muffin mix

1 (4-ounce) can chopped green chiles, drained

2 cups shredded cooked chicken breast (rotisserie), skin removed

1 (10-ounce) can red enchilada sauce

3/4 cup shredded reduced-fat Mexican-blend cheese

1 Preheat oven 400°F. Coat pie plate with nonstick cooking spray.

2 In bowl, combine milk, egg, 1 tablespoon taco seasoning, cream-style corn, corn muffin mix and green chiles, stirring just until moistened. Pour mixture into prepared pie plate. Bake 25–30 minutes.

3 In small bowl, toss chicken with remaining 1 tablespoon taco seasoning mix.

4 When cornbread is done (set and golden brown), remove from oven and pierce entire top with a fork (might stick to fork).

5 Carefully pour enchilada sauce over top. Top with chicken; sprinkle with cheese. Bake 10 minutes or until cheese melts.

TERRIFIC **TIP**

I think rotisserie chicken is the best invention ever for a favorite healthy time saving tip!

NUTRITION NUGGET

I used low-sodium creamed corn to reduce sodium but you don't have to use it. Low-sodium products are great for a healthier diet.

NUTRITIONAL INFORMATION Calories 271, Calories from Fat 22%, Fat 7 g, Saturated Fat 2 g, Cholesterol 60 mg, Sodium 720 mg, Carbohydrates 35 g, Dietary Fiber 2 g, Total Sugars 9 g, Protein 18 g
DIETARY EXCHANGES 2 1/2 starch, 2 lean meat

BEEF BRISKET

Two delicious dude meals in one! A few pantry-friendly ingredients make for a fall-apart-tender brisket. Turn leftovers into scrumptious brisket sliders and brisket quesadillas.

MAKES: 16 (4-5 ounce) servings · **PREP TIME:** 5 minutes · **COOK TIME:** About 6-8 hours ·

---

1 (5-6 pound) brisket
Garlic powder
1/3 cup light brown sugar
1 cup ketchup
2 envelopes dry onion soup mix
1 cup fat-free beef or chicken broth
1 onion, sliced

 TERRIFIC **TIP**

I like to add baby carrots and small potatoes or sweet potatoes.

1 Season brisket heavily with garlic powder. In 3 1/2–6-quart slow cooker, mix together brown sugar, ketchup, onion soup and broth.

2 Add brisket and turn to coat with sauce. Top with sliced onion.

3 Cook on LOW 6-8 hours or until tender.

4 *For Brisket Sliders:* Fill miniature rolls with brisket, Brie, and red onion—easy and fantastic!

For Brisket Quesadillas: Add brisket, sauce and your favorite cheese in between flour or corn tortillas.

NUTRITIONAL INFORMATION (FOR BRISKET) Calories 226, Calories from Fat 26%, Fat 6 g, Saturated Fat 2 g, Cholesterol 88 mg, Sodium 510 mg, Carbohydrates 11 g, Dietary Fiber 0 g, Total Sugars 9 g, Protein 30 g
DIETARY EXCHANGES 1/2 other carbohydrate, 4 lean meat

EASY MEAT SAUCE

Take a short cut with a jar of marinara and add fresh vegetables to amp up
the nutrition of this classic robust, hearty protein-packed meat sauce.

MAKES: 8 (1-cup) servings · **PREP TIME:** 15 minutes · **COOK TIME:** 30–35 minutes ·

---

1 onion, chopped

1 medium yellow squash, thinly
  sliced

1 medium zucchini, thinly sliced

2 pounds ground sirloin

1 tablespoon minced garlic

1 (24-ounce) jar marinara sauce

1 tablespoon dried basil leaves

1 tablespoon dried oregano leaves

Salt and pepper to taste

1 In large nonstick skillet coated with nonstick cooking spray, sauté onion, squash, and zucchini about 5 minutes. Add meat and garlic and cook over medium heat until meat is done and vegetables are tender, 5–7 minutes. Drain excess grease.

2 Add marinara, basil and oregano. Bring to boil, stirring constantly. Reduce heat, and simmer, uncovered, 20 minutes. Season to taste.

*Meat sauce freezes well in
individual zip-top freezer
bags to pull out for meals.*

*Eating high quality protein such
as lean meat at each meal may help
maintain muscle mass and boost
energy for an active lifestyle.*

*Serve over any
whole grain pasta.*

NUTRITIONAL INFORMATION Calories 220, Calories from fat 31%, Fat 8 g, Saturated Fat 3 g, Cholesterol 62 mg, Sodium 438 mg, Carbohydrate 12 g, Dietary Fiber 3 g, Sugars 3 g, Protein 27 g
DIETARY EXCHANGES 2 vegetable, 3 lean meat

PESTO SHRIMP

Perk up shrimp with pesto and tomatoes for a quick, insanely amazing meal.
Keep a jar of pesto sauce in your refrigerator for the best recipe shortcut!

MAKES: 4 servings · PREP TIME: 5 minutes · COOK TIME: 15 minutes ·

1 pound peeled medium shrimp

Salt and pepper to taste

1 tablespoon basil pesto (jarred)

1 tablespoon olive oil

1 pint cherry or Heirloom assorted
tomatoes

1/4 teaspoon red pepper flakes

1 Season shrimp to taste. In nonstick pan coated with nonstick cooking spray, heat pan and add shrimp cooking until done, about 5 minutes.

2 Toss with pesto and remove from heat.

3 Meanwhile, in another nonstick pan, heat olive oil. Add tomatoes, salt and pepper, and red pepper flakes, cooking until tomatoes begin to burst, smashing slightly while cooking, about 5–7 minutes. Add to shrimp.

TERRIFIC TIP

A jar of basil pesto is one of my favorite shortcuts. Try my White Spinach and Artichoke Pesto Pizza (page 122) or Pesto Potatoes (page 138). Basil Pesto quickly will become a favorite ingredient to toss into recipes for quick Italian flavor.

SERVING SUGGESTION

Serve savory seasoned pesto shrimp over polenta, pasta or rice or with toothpicks as an appetizer.

NUTRITIONAL INFORMATION Calories 170, Calories from Fat 32%, Fat 6 g, Saturated Fat 1 g, Cholesterol 184 mg, Sodium 179 mg, Carbohydrates 5 g, Dietary Fiber 1 g, Total Sugars 3 g, Protein 24 g
DIETARY EXCHANGES 1 vegetable, 3 lean meat

TACO PASTA SKILLET

Short on time but hungry? You'll ace dinner with this easy recipe!
Cook all the ingredients in one pan (yes, pasta too!) for a scrumptious southwestern one-dish meal.

MAKES: 12 (1-cup) servings · **PREP TIME:** 5 minutes · **COOK TIME:** 20–25 minutes ·

1 3/4 pounds ground sirloin

1 onion, chopped

1 tablespoon minced garlic

1 (1-ounce) package taco seasoning

1 (14 1/2-ounce) can fire-roasted diced tomatoes

1 (10-ounce) can tomatoes and green chilies

2 cups fat-free chicken broth

12 ounces rotini pasta

1 (15-ounce) can black beans, drained and rinsed

1 In large nonstick pan, cook meat, onion and garlic until meat is done. Add taco seasoning, diced tomatoes, tomatoes and green chilies and broth; bring to a boil

2 Add pasta stirring to combine. Return to boil, reduce heat, cover and cook about 10–14 minutes or until pasta is done. Stir in beans and heat.

Serve with avocado, shredded cheese and red onion.

NUTRITIONAL INFORMATION Calories 249, Calories from Fat 15%, Fat 4 g, Saturated Fat 1 g, Cholesterol 36 mg, Sodium 628 mg, Carbohydrates 32 g, Dietary Fiber 4 g, Total Sugars 3 g, Protein 21 g
DIETARY EXCHANGES 2 starch, 1 vegetable, 2 1/2 lean meat

STUFFED ARTICHOKE CASSEROLE

Dazzle everyone with this one skillet dish that actually tastes just like a stuffed artichoke.
But, the best part of this fabulous no-fuss recipe is there's no stuffing artichokes involved.

MAKES: 6 (2/3-cup) servings · **PREP TIME:** 10 minutes · **COOK TIME:** 15 minutes ·

---

1 tablespoon olive oil

1 large onion, chopped

1 teaspoon minced garlic

2 1/2 cups seasoned stuffing mix

1 teaspoon dried oregano leaves

1 teaspoon dried basil leaves

1 cup fat-free chicken broth

1 (14-ounce) can artichoke hearts, drained and coarsely chopped

1/4–1/3 cup grated Parmesan cheese

1 In large nonstick skillet, heat oil and sauté onion and garlic until tender, about 5–7 minutes.

2 Add stuffing, oregano and basil, mixing until combined. Stir in chicken broth and artichokes, carefully mixing.

3 Add cheese stirring until heated and well mixed.

Prepare ahead of time and transfer to baking dish. Heat in 350°F oven 20 minutes or until heated

For vegetarian version, substitute vegetable broth.

NUTRITIONAL INFORMATION Calories 144, Calories from Fat 39%, Fat 6 g, Saturated Fat 2 g, Cholesterol 4 mg, Sodium 506 mg, Carbohydrates 17 g, Dietary Fiber 2 g, Total Sugars 3 g, Protein 5 g
DIETARY EXCHANGES 1 starch, 1 vegetable, 1 fat

PULL APART BREAD

When you bring this buttery homemade bread made with cans of crescent rolls, butter and a Bundt pan to a party, you will be everyone's BFF! Don't have a Bundt pan? Get one to have for this recipe.

MAKES: 12–16 servings · **PREP TIME:** 5 minutes · **COOK TIME:** 19–23 minutes ·

---

2 tablespoons butter, melted

3 (8-ounce) cans reduced-fat crescent rolls

1 Preheat oven 375°F.

2 Pour butter into bottom of nonstick Bundt pan. Unroll crescent rolls and roll up individually. Layer on top butter overlapping rolls.

3 Bake 19–23 minutes or until top is golden brown. Immediately invert onto serving plate.

From soups to meats, this bread pairs well with just about any meal!

Use different shaped Bundt pans for a fun presentation.

NUTRITIONAL INFORMATION Calories 149, Calories from Fat 47%, Fat 8 g, Saturated Fat 4 g, Cholesterol 4 mg, Sodium 347 mg, Carbohydrates 18 g, Dietary Fiber 0 g, Total Sugars 3 g, Protein 3 g
DIETARY EXCHANGES 1 starch, 1 1/2 fat

CHOCOLATE CHIP CHEESECAKE BARS

Do you like cheesecake and chocolate chip cookies? With only four ingredients,
you get the most indulgent cheesecake bar cookie. Baking has never been so simple.

MAKES: 48 bars · **PREP TIME:** 10 minutes · **COOK TIME:** 25–30 minutes ·

1 (16.5-ounce) roll plus 4 ounces of another chocolate chip slice-and-bake cookie dough

1 (8-ounce) package reduced-fat cream cheese

2/3 cup sugar

1 teaspoon vanilla extract

2 egg whites

1 Preheat oven 350°F. Coat 13×9×2-inch baking pan with nonstick cooking spray.

2 Press one cookie dough roll into bottom of pan; set aside.

3 In mixing bowl, beat cream cheese, sugar and vanilla until creamy. Add egg whites, mixing well. Carefully pour on top cookie crust. Crumble remaining 4 ounces cookie dough over cream cheese layer. Bake 25–30 minutes or until filling is set.

 TERRIFIC **TIP**

Lots of options! Use extra chocolate chip cookie dough for cookies later or make this recipe without the extra cookie dough topping for a cheesecake bar. Or, crumble extra chocolate chip cookie dough on top for more of a cookie topping.

NUTRITIONAL INFORMATION Calories 80, Calories from Fat 42%, Fat 4 g, Saturated Fat 2 g, Cholesterol 6 mg, Sodium 61 mg, Carbohydrates 10 g, Dietary Fiber 0 g, Total Sugars 8 g, Protein 1 g
DIETARY EXCHANGES 1/2 other carbohydrate, 1 fat

CHOCOLATE GAME DAY COOKIE CAKE

Game on! No matter which team colors you support with M&M's, this is a Super Bowl-winning recipe.
Popular with all ages and I think this is quicker than making cookies.

MAKES: 24 pieces · **PREP TIME:** 10 minutes · **COOK TIME:** 15–20 minutes ·

1/2 cup butter

1 cup sugar

1 egg

1 teaspoon vanilla extract

1 1/2 cups all-purpose flour

1/4 cup cocoa

1/2 teaspoon baking soda

3/4 cup candy-coated milk chocolate candies

1 1/2 cups miniature marshmallows

1 Preheat oven 350°F. Coat 12–14-inch pizza pan with nonstick cooking spray.

2 In large mixing bowl, beat together butter and sugar until fluffy. Add egg and vanilla, blending well.

3 In small bowl, combine flour, cocoa, and baking soda. Gradually add to sugar mixture, blending until well mixed.

4 Spread dough on prepared pan, spreading dough to within 1 inch of edge of pan. Sprinkle dough with candies and marshmallows. Bake 15–20 minutes, or until edges are set. Don't overbake.

Use seasonal candies to keep in the holiday spirit on Halloween, Christmas, Valentine's Day, and Easter.

I like to add coconut and pecans before baking as an option.

NUTRITIONAL INFORMATION Calories 144, Calories from Fat 35%, Fat 6 g, Saturated Fat 3 g, Cholesterol 19 mg, Sodium 70 mg, Carbohydrates 22 g, Dietary Fiber 1 g, Total Sugars 14 g, Protein 2 g
DIETARY EXCHANGES 1 1/2 other carbohydrate, 1 fat

PISTACHIO ICE CREAM PIE

Yes, you can fix this dynamic dessert and appear "fancy!" Pick up at the store a chocolate crust, ice cream, pistachio pudding, and chocolate topping, for a frozen creamy melt-in-your-mouth bite of decadence.

MAKES: 10 servings · **PREP TIME:** 15 minutes · **COOK TIME:** 10 minutes ·

---

1 1/2 cup crushed chocolate graham crackers

3 tablespoons butter, melted

1/4 cup chopped shelled pistachios

1 quart fat-free vanilla ice cream or frozen yogurt, softened

1 (4-serving) dry instant pistachio-flavored pudding and pie filling mix

1/2 cup chocolate fat-free fudge topping, warmed

1 Preheat oven 375°F.

2 In 9-inch pie plate, stir together graham cracker crumbs, and butter, press on bottom and up sides. Bake 8–10 minutes. Cool completely.

3 Meanwhile, in a large bowl, quickly combine pistachios, ice cream, and instant pudding mix. Transfer mixture into cooled crust. Freeze, covered, at least 4 hours or until firm. Serve with warmed chocolate fudge topping on each slice.

Take a short cut and use a prepared chocolate crust from the grocery.

Did you know pistachios contain a higher amount of protein and lower amount of fat content in comparison to other nuts?

NUTRITIONAL INFORMATION Calories 257, Calories from Fat 21%, Fat 6 g, Saturated Fat 3 g, Cholesterol 9 mg, Sodium 341 mg, Carbohydrates 47 g, Dietary Fiber 1 g, Total Sugars 29 g, Protein 6 g

DIETARY EXCHANGES 3 other carbohydrate, 1 fat

CHOCOLATE TOFFEE TRIFLE

You'll fall in love with trifles because they're easy to make, can be made ahead of time and make an amazing presentation. A standing ovation kind of dessert! Layers of angel food cake, chocolate sauce, toffee, pudding and whipped topping can't be beat!

MAKES: 20 (2/3-cup) servings · **PREP TIME:** 15 minutes · **COOK TIME:** 5 minutes ·

1/2 cup sugar

3 tablespoons cocoa

1 tablespoon cornstarch

1 (5-ounce) can evaporated skimmed milk

1/4 cup coffee liqueur

3 (4-serving) packages instant vanilla pudding and pie filling mix

3 1/2 cups skim milk

1 (16-ounce) angel food cake (bought at store), cubed

3 bananas, peeled and sliced

3 (1.4-ounce) chocolate-covered toffee candy bars, crushed

1 (12-ounce) container fat-free frozen whipped topping, thawed

1 In small nonstick pot, combine sugar, cocoa, cornstarch, and evaporated milk. Bring to boil, lower heat and cook until thickened. Remove from heat; add coffee liqueur. Cool.

2 In large bowl, whisk pudding mix and skim milk together until thickened.

4 In trifle dish, layer angel food cake, pudding, bananas, toffee, drizzle chocolate sauce and whipped topping. Repeat layers, ending with whipped topping. Refrigerate until serving.

Sprinkle any extra toffee candy bars on top the trifle and garnish with fresh berries.

Don't worry about making the layers even as I promise it will look spectacular. You can always buy chocolate sauce instead of making it.

NUTRITIONAL INFORMATION Calories 247, Calories from Fat 9%, Fat 2 g, Saturated Fat 1 g, Cholesterol 3 mg, Sodium 442 mg, Carbohydrates 51 g, Dietary Fiber 1 g, Total Sugars 31 g, Protein 4 g
DIETARY EXCHANGES 3 1/2 other carbohydrate

CHICKEN JAMBALAYA

A great one-pot dish to feed the group on game day or even dinner on a day you don't want to cook.
Flavorful and surprisingly simple in a slow cooker.

MAKES: 8 (1 1/2-cup) servings · **PREP TIME:** 10 minutes · **COOK TIME:** About 3 hours ·

1 pound boneless, skinless chicken breast, cut into chunks

1/2 pound reduced-fat sausage, sliced

1 cup chopped celery

1 large onion, chopped

1 large green pepper, cored and chopped

1 teaspoon minced garlic

1/2 teaspoon dried thyme leaves

1 (14 1/2-ounce) can diced fire-roasted tomatoes

2 cups fat-free chicken broth

2 tablespoons tomato paste

Salt and pepper to taste

2 cups instant brown rice

1/2 cup chopped green onions

1 In 3 1/2–6-quart slow cooker, place chicken and sausage. Add remaining ingredients except brown rice and green onions.

2 Cover and cook on LOW 2 1/2 hours. Turn to HIGH and stir in rice. Cover, and cook 30 minutes more or until rice is tender and liquid absorbed. Stir in green onions.

NUGGET

Use low-sodium chicken broth to cut sodium for a diabetic-friendly recipe.

TERRIFIC TIP

Sometimes you can find a healthier version turkey Andouille sausage.

Tired of wasting tomato paste, look for it in a tube—squeeze out desired amount. Purchase prechopped ingredients for a short cut.

NUTRITIONAL INFORMATION Calories 220, Calories from Fat 13%, Fat 3 g, Saturated Fat 1 g, Cholesterol 46 mg, Sodium 652 mg, Carbohydrates 28 g, Dietary Fiber 3 g, Total Sugars 6 g, Protein 19 g
DIETARY EXCHANGES 1 1/2 starch, 1 vegetable, 2 1/2 lean meat

PULLED CHICKEN CROCK POT

One of my favorite go to chicken recipes for a fix and forget it meal.
Love the versatility of pulled chicken for sandwiches, sliders or an entrée.

MAKES: 10 (1/2-cup) servings · **PREP TIME:** 5–10 minutes · **COOK TIME:** About 6 hours ·

---

1 cup chopped onion

1 tablespoon minced garlic

2 tablespoons cider vinegar

1 (12-ounce) bottle chili sauce

1 tablespoon light brown sugar

1/2 teaspoon ground cumin

1/8 teaspoon ground ginger

1/2 cup fat-free chicken broth

2 pounds boneless, skinless
   chicken breasts

1 In 3 1/2–6-quart slow cooker, combine all ingredients except chicken in slow cooker.

2 Add chicken and turn to coat. Cover and cook on HIGH about 6 hours or until chicken is tender.

2 Remove chicken breasts and shred with two forks. Return shredded chicken to crock pot.

Chili sauce is found where ketchup is in the grocery. If you want to substitute ketchup for chili sauce, add 1 teaspoon chili powder to ketchup.

NUTRITIONAL INFORMATION Calories 148, Calories from Fat 15%, Fat 2 g, Saturated Fat 1 g, Cholesterol 58 mg, Sodium 613 mg, Carbohydrates 11 g, Dietary Fiber 0 g, Total Sugars 8 g, Protein 20 g
DIETARY EXCHANGES 1/2 other carbohydrate, 3 lean meat

SLOW COOKER SALMON

The slow cooker solves the time issue of waiting and watching salmon. Put it on for 2 hours and impress with a personal packet of moist salmon with wonderful sweet savory seasoning. Yes, it really works!

MAKES: 4 servings • **PREP TIME:** 10 minutes • **COOK TIME:** 2 hours •

4 (4–6-ounce) pieces salmon, skinned removed

4 large squares heavy duty foil

2 tablespoons light brown sugar

1 teaspoon paprika

1 teaspoon ground cumin

1/2 teaspoon garlic powder

1/2 teaspoon dried oregano leaves

Salt to taste

1/4 teaspoon cayenne pepper

1 Lay each piece of salmon in center of piece of foil twice size of salmon. In small bowl, mix together all the seasonings. Top salmon with seasoning. Bring up sides of foil over salmon so edges meet and crimp to make contained packet.

2 In 3 1/2–6-quart slow cooker, put foil packets into dry slow cooker. Cover and cook on HIGH about 2 hours or until salmon flakes with fork.

Serve with brown rice or quinoa and steamed or roasted vegetables like Brussels Sprouts Stir-Fry (page 124).

NUTRITION NUGGET

Get your protein from fish, and remember protein helps boost muscles.

NUTRITIONAL INFORMATION Calories 179, Calories from Fat 27%, Fat 5 g, Saturated Fat 1 g, Cholesterol 53 mg, Sodium 90 mg, Carbohydrates 8 g, Dietary Fiber 0 g, Total Sugars 7 g, Protein 24 g
DIETARY EXCHANGES 1/2 other carbohydrate, 3 lean meat

BEEF STEW IN SLOW COOKER

Simple beef stew becomes a quick favorite with secret ingredient of
barbecue sauce combined with meat and lots of vegetables.

MAKES: 8 (1-cup) servings · **PREP TIME:** 15 minutes · **COOK TIME:** About 5–6 hours ·

1 1/2 pounds beef stew meat

2/3 cup sweet barbecue sauce

1 1/2 teaspoons paprika

2 cups butternut squash chunks

2 cups peeled sweet potato chunks

2 cups baby carrots

2 cups thickly sliced zucchini

2 cups thickly sliced yellow squash

1/2 cup water

1 In 3 1/2–6-quart slow cooker, add all ingredients. Cover and cook on HIGH 5–6 hours or until meat is tender.

*Use any combination of the
10 cups of vegetables.*

*I like to serve over
couscous or rice to soak
up all the super sauce.*

**NUTRITION
NUGGET**

*Only 3 ounces of lean
beef contains 10 essential
nutrients and half the daily
value of protein, 25 grams and
only about 150 calories.*

NUTRITIONAL INFORMATION Calories 231, Calories from Fat 25%, Fat 6 g, Saturated Fat 2 g, Cholesterol 53 mg, Sodium 211 mg, Carbohydrates 24 g, Dietary Fiber 3 g, Total Sugars 13 g, Protein 18 g

DIETARY EXCHANGES 1 vegetable, 1 starch, 1/2 other carbohydrate, 2 1/2 lean meat

BEEF FAJITAS IN SLOW COOKER

Fajitas have never been simpler! A quick fajita rub, combined with salsa, peppers and onions in slow cooker for fall-apart tender fajitas.

MAKES: 8 (about 1/2 cup meat) servings · **PREP TIME:** 10 minutes · **COOK TIME:** About 5-8 hours ·

1 (16-ounce) jar salsa

1 tablespoon chili powder

1 tablespoons ground cumin

1 tablespoon paprika

1 tablespoon garlic powder

Salt and pepper to taste

2 pounds flank steak, skirt steak or boneless chuck

1 large onion, sliced

3 assorted bell peppers, cored and sliced (any combination green, red, yellow)

1 In 3 1/2–6-quart slow cooker, pour salsa on bottom.

2 In small bowl, mix chili powder, cumin, paprika, garlic powder and season to taste. Rub meat with seasoning mixture. Add meat to slow cooker with remaining seasoning, onion and peppers.

3 Cover and cook on LOW 8 hours, or HIGH 5–6 hours or until tender. Use slotted spoon, to remove meat, onions and pepper.

Serve with your favorite condiments and tortillas.

Use corn tortillas to keep gluten-free.

Bell peppers are loaded with antioxidents and one of the best sources of vitamin C.

NUTRITIONAL INFORMATION Calories 211, Calories from Fat 41%, Fat 9 g, Saturated Fat 4 g, Cholesterol 48 mg, Sodium 288 mg, Carbohydrates 10 g, Dietary Fiber 2 g, Total Sugars 5 g, Protein 20 g
DIETARY EXCHANGES 2 vegetable, 3 lean meat

PORK TENDERLOIN WITH RASPBERRY CHIPOTLE SAUCE

Talk about an unbeatable pork tenderloin—a knock it out of the park recipe done effortlessly!

MAKES: 6 (4-ounce) servings · PREP TIME: 5 minutes · COOK TIME: About 4 hours ·

2 (1-pound) pork tenderloins, trimmed

2 tablespoons minced garlic

1 tablespoon dried thyme leaves

3/4 cup Raspberry Chipotle Sauce, divided

1 In 3 1/2–6-quart slow cooker, season pork tenderloins with garlic and thyme. Add 1/4 cup Raspberry Chipotle sauce.

2 Cover and cook on LOW 4–6 hours or until tender.

3 Preheat broiler. Remove tenderloins to foil lined baking pan. Spread 1/4 cup Raspberry Chipotle Sauce over both tenderloins.

4 Broil 1–2 minutes, turn over and cover tenderloins with remaining 1/4 cup Raspberry Chipotle Sauce. Broil again 1–2 minutes.

Look for Raspberry Chipotle Sauce with barbecue sauces in the grocery. If they don't have it, find a comparable flavor.

NUTRITIONAL INFORMATION Calories 242, Calories from Fat 15%, Fat 4 g, Saturated Fat 1 g, Cholesterol 79 mg, Sodium 183 mg, Carbohydrates 21 g, Dietary Fiber 2 g, Total Sugars 18 g, Protein 29 g

DIETARY EXCHANGES 1 1/2 other carbohydrate, 4 lean meat

EASY POT ROAST

A roast like grandma makes but now you can make it too! A homemade meal that basically cooks itself—throw in a low-temperature oven or crock pot and have this protein-packed dinner waiting when you get home!

MAKES: 14 (4 ounces beef + 1/2 cup vegetables) servings · **PREP TIME:** 10 minutes · **COOK TIME:** 4–6 hours ·

1 (4-pound) beef sirloin tip roast,
trimmed of excess fat

6 cloves garlic, sliced or garlic
powder

Salt and pepper to taste

1 large onion, sliced

1 envelope onion soup mix

1 cup beef broth

1 (16-ounce) package baby carrots

1 sweet potato, peeled,
cut into chunks

2 red potatoes, peeled,
cut into chunks

1 Preheat oven 300° F. Cut slits in roast, stuff pieces of garlic throughout meat.

2 Season meat to taste. Place meat in oven-proof pot. Cover with sliced onion, top with onion soup mix and beef broth.

3 Cover, bake 4 hours depending on size of roast. Add carrots and potatoes, continue cooking another hour or until meat is tender.

*Slow cooker instructions:
In 3 1/2–6-quart slow
cooker, follow directions
above and cook on LOW
6–8 hours or until tender.*

*These few ingredients
create a sensational gravy
that's great over brown
rice or barley.*

NUTRITIONAL INFORMATION Calories 235, Calories from Fat 30%, Fat 8 g, Saturated Fat 2 g, Cholesterol 79 mg, Sodium 280 mg, Carbohydrates 11 g, Dietary Fiber 2 g, Total Sugars 4 g, Protein 29 g
DIETARY EXCHANGES 1 vegetable, 1/2 starch, 4 lean meat

GRILLING & HUNTING

GRILLING & HUNTING
COOKING FOR THE OUTDOORS

WHAT FIRES YOU UP?
IS GRILLING A GUY THING?
IS WILD GAME GOOD FOR YOU?

Grilling has been an American favorite past time for as long as I can remember, and the grill has the reputation of being the guy's cooking turf. Often, casual entertaining revolves around the grill with good food and lots of fun stories. Whether you have a green egg, charcoal or gas grill, everyone has their own grilling technique. Is it the grilling experience, the marinades, the smoky taste or just seeing those grill lines on the food that intrigues men with their grill? I have it all in this chapter with fantastic marinades, creative grilling recipes and some of the best grilling tips to make you the top dog griller!

Whatever the meat, it's the marinade that really adds to the flavor and tenderness! Marinades are the key to a tasty meat—usually made up of a mixture of oil, vinegar, herbs and spices. Along with vinegar, lemon juice and wine are other popular acidic marinade ingredients that adds to the flavor and tenderizes tough meat by breaking down tissue for a moister, juicy meat.

Actually, grilling can be a healthier choice in cooking—much better than deep frying and food with heavy sauces. So, let's get grilling!

- Keep food in refrigerator until ready to grill.
- Preheat your grill to start with a hot grill.
- Turn food with tongs and don't stab food as it lets out the juices.
- Let food rest on plate about 5 minutes before serving to let juices redistribute.
- Boneless chicken does fine over direct heat but bone-in pieces need indirect heat as they take longer to grill.
- Use a meat thermometer to check for doneness.

Hunting

Lions, tigers, and bears—oh my! Well, these aren't exactly wild game choices, traditional wild game such as venison, dove, and bison may not be so scary after all. Both traditional animal meats, such as beef from farm raised cows and wild game, such as venison are both high in protein and low in carbohydrates; however wild game nutritional content varies from farm raised meat due to their more active lifestyle, contributing to leaner profiles. Although animal meat is usually high in saturated fat, wild game is often low in saturated fat. Because wild game is lower in fat, they are also lower in calories and cholesterol than farm-raised beef. The way that wild game is raised, with natural, plant based diets also add to their health benefits of higher anti-inflammatory omega fatty acids as opposed to pro-inflammatory grain or corn-fed beef.

Common Lean Wild Game:

- Venison
- Dove
- Quail
- Rabbit
- Bison

SOUTHWESTERN MARINADE

Between a marinade and a rub, this southwestern infused mixture really flavors your meat.
Skirt steak or flank steak may be used.

2 tablespoons olive oil
1/4 cup lime juice
1/4 cup orange juice
1 tablespoon honey
1/2 cup chopped red onion
1/4 cup chopped cilantro
1 tablespoon minced garlic
1 teaspoon chili powder
1 teaspoon ground cumin
1 teaspoon ground paprika
Salt and pepper to taste

1 In large plastic zip-top resealable bag, combine all ingredients except meat and mix together.

2 Add meat and marinate in refrigerator 1 hour or overnight, time permitted. Pan sear or grill as desired.

 SERVING SUGGESTION *Sauté some peppers and onions, pick up some condiments for the best fajitas.*

QUICK MEAT MARINADE

This is the "bomb" when it comes to meat marinades. Flank steak, tenderloins,
or any favorite meat, this quick marinade perks up the taste!

1/4 cup balsamic vinegar
1/4 cup low-sodium soy sauce
1 cup Worcestershire sauce
1 tablespoon Dijon mustard
1 tablespoon molasses

1 In bowl or plastic zip-top resealable bag combine all ingredients.

2 Add meat and refrigerate until ready to grill.

QUICK GRILLED VEGETABLE MARINADE

Give veggies a grilled smoky flavor with this quick marinade. Cut larger vegetables into
smaller pieces and skewer sliced veggies or cherry tomatoes into shish kebobs.

1/3 cup fat-free Italian dressing
2 tablespoons low-sodium soy sauce
1 tablespoon grated fresh ginger
Onion slices, zucchini wedges, squash
wedges, tomatoes

1 In plastic zip-top resealable bag or glass dish, combine all ingredients. Marinate 30 minutes for larger vegetables, 15 minutes for smaller, time permitting.

2 Coat grill with nonstick cooking spray and grill vegetables until desired doneness over medium heat. Smaller vegetables cook quicker and larger ones require more time.

 TERRIFIC TIP *Good grilling vegetables include: corn, portabella mushrooms, onions, bell peppers, zucchini, eggplant, asparagus and tomatoes.*

JAMAICAN JERK CHICKEN MARINADE

The Jamaican Jerk flavor makes this chicken marinade a home run recipe.

2 green onions, chopped

1 jalapeño pepper, seeded and
   coarsely chopped

1 tablespoon minced fresh ginger

2 tablespoons seasoned rice vinegar

2 tablespoons Worcestershire sauce

1 teaspoon olive oil

1 teaspoon ground allspice

1 teaspoon dried thyme

Salt and pepper to taste

1 In blender or food processor, process all ingredients until mixed.

2 In plastic zip-top resealable bag or glass dish, combine mixture and chicken, to marinate. Refrigerate one hour.

 SERVING SUGGESTION *Use marinade for chicken shish kebobs. The pineapple, mushrooms and peppers complement the spicy chicken.*

 TERRIFIC TIP *Jamaican jerk seasoning adds a spicy flavor to dishes— "jerking" originated as an old Jamaican method for preserving and cooking meats.*

BEST BEER SALMON

If you're drinking beer while grilling, you might as well cook with it!
Try this easy moist salmon poached in a sensational mixture cooked in a foil pouch.
That means no washing dishes—eat straight out of the foil to enjoy the juices.

MAKES: 4 servings · **PREP TIME:** 10 minutes · **COOK TIME:** 15 minutes ·

4 (6-ounce) salmon fillets,
   skin removed

4 large squares heavy duty foil

1 teaspoon garlic salt, divided

4 thin slices onion rings

4 teaspoons olive oil, divided

4 teaspoons light brown sugar,
   divided

8 tablespoons lite beer, divided

1 Place each salmon fillet in middle of large foil square. Sprinkle each with 1/4 teaspoon garlic salt, top with one sliced onion, 1 teaspoon olive oil, and 1 teaspoon brown sugar.

2 Pour 2 tablespoons beer around each fillet, not on top of salmon. Fold up foil into pouches.

3 Grill 15 minutes until salmon flakes easily with a fork and eat directly out of the foil.

 TERRIFIC TIP *Cook in the oven at 400°F for 15 minutes.*

NUTRITIONAL INFORMATION Calories 286, Calories from Fat 39%, Fat 12 g, Saturated Fat 2 g, Cholesterol 80 mg, Sodium 372 mg, Carbohydrates 5 g, Dietary Fiber 0 g, Total Sugars 5 g, Protein 36 g
DIETARY EXCHANGES 1/2 other carbohydrate, 5 lean meat

CEDAR PLANK SALMON

Take grilling to another level with this delicious Asian-marinated salmon on cedar plank.

MAKES: 4 servings · **PREP TIME:** 5 minutes + cedar plank soaking time · **COOK TIME:** 20 minutes ·

2–3 untreated cedar planks

1 tablespoon canola oil

1 tablespoon seasoned rice vinegar

1 teaspoon sesame oil

1/4 cup low-sodium soy sauce

1/2 cup chopped green onions

1 tablespoon grated fresh ginger

1 tablespoon minced garlic

4 (4–5 ounce) salmon fillets,
  skin removed

1 Soak cedar planks in water for two-three hours. Helps prevent burning on the grill.

2 In plastic zip-top resealable bag or glass dish, combine oil, vinegar, sesame oil, soy sauce, green onions, ginger and garlic. Place salmon in marinade, turn to coat and marinate 1 hour.

3 Preheat grill to medium heat. Place planks on grill and when they start to smoke, place salmon on planks. Baste with marinade half way through cooking and then discard remaining marinade.

4 Close grill and cook about 15–20 minutes or until salmon is done and flakes easily with fork. Remove from grill and let sit 5 minutes. Salmon will continue to cook on cedar plank.

Put cedar planks in pan of water with cup to hold it down in the morning and then you're ready to use them for dinner that night.

NUTRITIONAL INFORMATION Calories 168, Calories from Fat 35%, Fat 6 g, Saturated Fat 1 g, Cholesterol 53 mg, Sodium 477 mg, Carbohydrates 2 g, Dietary Fiber 0 g, Total Sugars 2 g, Protein 25 g

DIETARY EXCHANGES 3 lean meat

GRILLED SHRIMP

These shrimp will dominate the conversation, bursting with flavor from this simple citrus marinade.

MAKES: 6 servings · **PREP TIME:** 15 minutes · **COOK TIME:** 10–15 minutes ·

1/3 cup lime juice

1 tablespoon honey

2 tablespoons low-sodium soy sauce

2 tablespoons Worcestershire sauce

1 cup orange juice

1 tablespoon minced garlic

2 pounds peeled large shrimp

1 In plastic zip-top resealable bag or glass dish, mix lime juice, honey, soy sauce, Worcestershire sauce, orange juice, and garlic. Add shrimp, and marinate 15 minutes.

2 Grill shrimp on high heat, or broil in oven for several minutes on each side, or until done.

TERRIFIC TIP

Consider alternate methods of grill cleaning, such as crumpled up foil or a pumice stone instead of a wire bristle brush, to prevent dangerous breakage and wires getting stuck on the grill, then transferring to food.

SERVING SUGGESTION

Use shrimp in shish kabobs with vegetables.

NUTRITIONAL INFORMATION Calories 116, Calories from Fat 23%, Fat 1 g, Saturated Fat 0 g, Cholesterol 215 mg, Sodium 433 mg, Carbohydrates 1 g, Dietary Fiber 0 g, Total Sugars 3 g, Protein 23 g
DIETARY EXCHANGES 3 1/2 very lean meat

GRILLED SHRIMP MARGHERITA PIZZA

Men this is your chance to impress with the thrill of the grill with the rich grilled flavor of the shrimp, tomatoes and onion. Chris, thanks for sharing this spectacular pizza recipe with me!

MAKES: 8 servings · PREP TIME: 10 minutes + marinade time · COOK TIME: 15–20 minutes ·

2/3 cup medium peeled shrimp

2 cups cherry tomatoes

1 medium onion, sliced 1/2 inch thick

1/3 cup fat-free Italian dressing

Skewers

1 thin pizza crust

2 tablespoons olive oil

1 cup shredded part-skim
   mozzarella cheese

2 tablespoons fresh chopped basil

1 Marinate shrimp, tomatoes and onion in Italian dressing 30 minutes, time permitting. Skewer shrimp and tomatoes separately and put onion slices directly on grill, discard marinade.

2 Coat grill with nonstick cooking spray. Cook shrimp about 3–6 minutes, turning until shrimp are done. Cook tomatoes on high about 2–3 minutes or until begin to pop. Cook onions on high about 5 minutes, turning. Remove; set aside.

3 Coat each side of pizza crust with olive oil. Grill one side pizza crust on medium high about 2 minutes, flip and turn grill to low. Top with cheese, grilled shrimp, tomatoes and onion. Continue cooking about 2 minutes or until cheese melted. Remove from heat and sprinkle with basil.

If using wooden skewers, soak them in water before using to prevent burning.

This pizza works great with fresh dough or pizza dough in a can. Be sure to oil the dough to keep it from sticking.

Leave out the shrimp for the most perfect Margherita pizza.

NUTRITIONAL INFORMATION Calories 210, Calories from Fat 38%, Fat 9 g, Saturated Fat 3 g, Cholesterol 42 mg, Sodium 400 mg, Carbohydrates 20 g, Dietary Fiber 2 g, Total Sugars 4 g, Protein 13 g
DIETARY EXCHANGES 1 starch, 1 vegetable, 1 1/2 lean meat, 1 fat

CHICKEN THIGHS IN HONEY SRIRACHA SAUCE

Stay home and turn to the grill for your favorite buffalo wing flavor with Sriracha sauce, honey and lime juice. This chicken kicks it up a notch!

MAKES: 6 servings · PREP TIME: 5 minutes + marinate time · COOK TIME: 15–20 minutes ·

1/2 cup plus 2 tablespoons sriracha sauce, divided

2 tablespoons honey

6 boneless, skinless chicken thighs (about 2 pounds)

3 tablespoons lime juice

3 tablespoons chopped fresh cilantro

1 In small bowl, mix together 2 tablespoons sriracha sauce and honey; set aside.

2 Place chicken in plastic zip-top resealable bag or glass dish. Add remaining sriracha sauce and lime juice to chicken. Coat chicken and let stand 15 minutes.

3 Spray grill with nonstick cooking spray and preheat to medium. Place chicken on grill and sear on medium high on both sides. Continue cooking on indirect heat around 15–20 minutes or until chicken is done (170°F) turning several times.

4 Transfer chicken to platter, brush with reserved sriracha-honey sauce mixture, cover, let stand 5 minutes. Sprinkle with cilantro.

Sriracha is a type of hot sauce made from chili peppers, vinegar, garlic, sugar and salt.

NUTRITIONAL INFORMATION Calories 216, Calories from Fat 27%, Fat 6 g, Saturated Fat 2 g, Cholesterol 144 mg, Sodium 435 mg, Carbohydrates 9 g, Dietary Fiber 0 g, Total Sugars 9 g, Protein 29 g
DIETARY EXCHANGES 1/2 other carbohydrate, 4 lean meat

FLANK STEAK IN COFFEE MARINADE

Coffee adds depth and flavor while being a natural tenderizer for a rich, flavorsome meat.
Save some of your morning coffee for the marinade and toss on grill when get home.

MAKES: 6 servings · PREP TIME: 5 minutes + marinate time · COOK TIME: 15 minutes ·

1 cup strong black coffee

1 tablespoon Dijon mustard

1 teaspoon minced garlic

2 tablespoons balsamic vinegar

2 tablespoons light brown sugar

1 teaspoon olive oil

Salt and pepper to taste

2 pounds flank steak, trimmed of fat

1 In large plastic zip-top resealable bag or glass dish, combine all ingredients except flank steak, mixing well. Add flank steak, refrigerate, and marinate 2 hours or more, turning occasionally.

2 Discard marinade. Grill over high heat until cooked rare to medium rare, 4–7 minutes on each side.

3 Serve rare, cut diagonally across grain into thin slices. Let sit 5 minutes before slicing.

NUTRITIONAL INFORMATION Calories 211, Calories from Fat 40%, Fat 9 g, Saturated Fat 4 g, Cholesterol 86 mg, Sodium 86 mg, Carbohydrates 0 g, Dietary Fiber 0 g, Total Sugars 0 g, Protein 30 g

DIETARY EXCHANGES 4 lean meat

HONEY GINGER PORK TENDERLOIN

Orange juice, honey and Asian seasonings are the perfect marinade mate for pork tenderloins.

MAKES: 6–8 servings · PREP TIME: 5 minutes + marinate time · COOK TIME: 20–25 minutes ·

1/4 cup orange juice

1/4 cup low-sodium soy sauce

3 tablespoons honey

1 tablespoon chopped garlic

1/2 teaspoon pepper

1/2 teaspoon dry mustard

1/2 teaspoon ground ginger

1/2 teaspoon onion powder

2 (1-pound) pork tenderloins, trimmed of fat

1 In shallow glass dish or plastic zip-top resealable bag, combine all ingredients except tenderloins. Add pork tenderloins.

2 Marinate in refrigerator at least 4 hours (time permitting) or overnight. Grill over medium-high heat, 20–25 minutes.

3 *To prepare in oven:* Bake 350°F, basting with marinade mixture, 50 minutes, or until meat thermometer registers 160°F. Discard unused marinade.

 The best way to test pork's doneness is with a meat thermometer. Cutting it to check on doneness lets too many good juices run out.

NUTRITIONAL INFORMATION Calories 136, Calories from Fat 17%, Fat 2 g, Saturated Fat 1 g, Cholesterol 74 mg, Sodium 255 mg, Carbohydrates 2 g, Dietary Fiber 0 g, Total Sugars 3 g, Protein 24 g

DIETARY EXCHANGES 3 lean meat

DOVE BREAST POPPERS

A hunter's popular dove or quail simple recipe.

MAKES: 6 (5-piece) servings · **PREP TIME:** 15 minutes + marinate time · **COOK TIME:** 15–20 minutes ·

30 boneless dove breasts, halved

1 1/2 cups reduced-fat Italian dressing

2 tablespoons Worcestershire sauce

2 fresh jalapeños, cored and sliced lengthwise

1 (8-ounce) package reduced-fat cream cheese

7 1/2 slices center-cut bacon, cut in half

1 In plastic zip-top resealable bag or glass dish, marinate dove breasts in Italian dressing and Worcestershire sauce in refrigerator overnight or at least 8 hours. Discard marinade.

2 Lay dove breast on plate and place jalapeño slice and about 1 tablespoon cream cheese on top dove. Wrap together with half of bacon slice and secure with toothpick. Repeat with remaining dove breasts.

3 Grill over medium heat about 15–20 minutes or until bacon crisp and dove done. Watch carefully—bacon can cause flames to flare.

 This recipe may be used for quail, duck, or goose breasts. Use only small pieces.

NUTRITIONAL INFORMATION Calories 355, Calories from Fat 44%, Fat 15 g, Saturated Fat 7 g, Cholesterol 171 mg, Sodium 812 mg, Carbohydrates 2 g, Dietary Fiber 0 g, Total Sugars 2 g, Protein 40 g

DIETARY EXCHANGES 5 lean meat

VENISON ROAST

Nothing beats a good venison roast with delicious gravy.

MAKES: 12 servings · **PREP TIME:** 15 minutes · **COOK TIME:** 3 hours ·

3–4 pound venison roast, trimmed

4 garlic cloves, peeled and sliced

2 tablespoons Creole seasoning

Flour to coat

1/4 cup canola oil

2 (10.5-ounce) cans French Onion soup plus 2 cans of water

2 baking potatoes, cut into chunks

1 cup baby carrots

1 Preheat oven 350° F.

2 Make slits in roast with knife and insert garlic. Season roast with Creole seasoning and dust with flour.

3 In large roasting pot, heat oil and brown roast on all sides. Remove roast from pan, discard excess oil and return roast to pot. Add soup and 2 cans water.

4 Bake, covered, 3 hours or until tender. Add potatoes and carrots and continue baking another hour or until vegetables are tender.

NUTRITIONAL INFORMATION Calories 209, Calories from Fat 26%, Fat 6 g, Saturated Fat 2 g, Cholesterol 98 mg, Sodium 320 mg, Carbohydrates 10 g, Dietary Fiber 1 g, Total Sugars 2 g, Protein 28 g

DIETARY EXCHANGES 1/2 starch, 3 lean meat

VENISON CHILI

This hearty chili recipe will satisfy all you ravenous hunters.

MAKES: 8 (1-cup) servings · **PREP TIME:** 15 minutes · **COOK TIME:** 35–40 minutes ·

---

4 strips turkey bacon, diced

2 pounds ground venison

1 cup chopped onion

1 cup chopped green bell pepper

2 tablespoons minced garlic

1/2 (12-ounce) can lite beer

1/2 (6-ounce) can tomato paste

2 tablespoons chili powder

1 teaspoon ground cumin

1 teaspoon oregano leaves

1 teaspoon cayenne pepper or to taste

1 (14 1/2-ounce) can fire-roasted diced tomatoes

1 cup fat-free beef broth

1 (15-ounce) can black beans, rinsed and drained

Salt and pepper to taste

1 In large nonstick pot, cook bacon until done, about 5 minutes. Remove bacon to plate.

2 Add venison, onion, bell pepper and garlic and cook over medium heat until venison is done, about 7 minutes.

3 Stir in remaining ingredients. Bring mixture to a boil, reduce heat and cook, uncovered, 30 minutes or until mixture thickens.

SERVING SUGGESTION

Serve topped with chopped onion, shredded cheese and a dollop of plain yogurt.

TERRIFIC TIP

Venison sausage may be substituted for bacon. Add more beef broth if too thick. Can also be made with ground sirloin.

NUTRITIONAL INFORMATION Calories 256, Calories from Fat 15%, Fat 4 g, Saturated Fat 1 g, Cholesterol 106 mg, Sodium 581 mg, Carbohydrates 18 g, Dietary Fiber 5 g, Total Sugars 5 g, Protein 34 g

DIETARY EXCHANGES 2 vegetable, 1/2 starch, 4 lean meat

INDEX

PANTRY SHOPPING LIST

REFRIGERATOR STAPLES

Butter
Cheese (varieties, reduced-fat)
Reduced-fat cream cheese
Eggs
Fruit
Garlic (minced in jar, fresh)
Bell peppers
Lemon and lime juice
Mixed greens (baby spinach, kale)
Onion (yellow, red, and green)
Pizza dough
Refrigerated biscuits, crescent rolls
Skim milk
Rotisserie chicken
Turkey bacon
Vegetables
Yogurt, Greek and plain (nonfat or
   light)

PANTRY STAPLES

Biscuit baking mix
Bread (Hawaiian rolls)
Bread crumbs (Italian, plain, panko)
Couscous
Evaporated skimmed milk
Oils (canola, olive)
Pasta
Quinoa
Rice (Arborio, brown, white, wild,
   yellow)

BAKING STAPLES

Baking powder
Baking soda
Cake mixes (chocolate, yellow,
   brownie)
Semi-sweet chocolate chips
Cocoa
Cornstarch
Flour (all-purpose)
Instant pudding and pie filling mix
Nonstick cooking spray
Nuts
Oatmeal (old-fashioned)
Sugar (granulated, brown and
   confectioners')
Extracts (vanilla, almond)

CONDIMENT STAPLES

Hot sauce
Honey
Ketchup
Mayonnaise (light or low fat)
Mustard (creole, Dijon or yellow)
Marinara sauce (jars)
Peanut butter
Salad dressing (fat-free or reduced-fat)
Salsa
Soy sauce (low-sodium)
Vinegar (balsamic, seasoned rice,
   white and wine)
Worcestershire sauce

CANNED GOODS

Beans (assorted)
Olives (Kalamata sliced)
Broth (beef, chicken, vegetable)
Enchilada sauce
Green chilies (diced)
Tomatoes (diced, paste, sauce)
Diced tomatoes and green chilies

SPICE PANTRY STARTER LIST

Basil leaves
Chili powder
Cinnamon (ground)
Cumin (ground)
Curry powder
Garlic powder
Ginger (ground)
Oregano leaves
Paprika
Parsley flakes (dried)
Pepper (black, coarsely ground,
   red pepper flakes)
Salt
Thyme leaves

FROZEN PANTRY STAPLES

Chicken breasts
Pork tenderloins
Fish (salmon and all types)
Frozen veggies (spinach, corn,
   edamame)
Meat (ground, roast, flank steak)
Seafood (shrimp, crawfish)
Yogurt or ice cream (reduced-fat or
   fat-free)

MEASUREMENT EQUIVALENTS

3 teaspoons = 1 tablespoon
4 tablespoons = 1/4 cup
5 tablespoons + 1 teaspoon = 1/3 cup
8 tablespoons = 1/2 cup
12 tablespoons = 3/4 cup
16 tablespoons = 1 cup (8 ounces)
2 cups = 1 pint (16 ounces)
4 cups (2 pints) = 1 quart (32 ounces)
8 cups (4 pints) = 1/2 gallon (64 ounces)
4 quarts = 1 gallon (128 ounces)

SUBSTITUTIONS

1 tablespoon balsamic vinegar =
   1 tablespoon sherry or cider vinegar

Plain or Greek, fat-free or low fat yogurt
   for sour cream or buttermilk

1 cup buttermilk = 1 tablespoon lemon
   juice or vinegar plus milk to make
   1 cup

1 cup milk = 1/2 cup evaporated milk
   plus 1/2 cup water

1 cup yogurt = 1 cup sour cream

1 cup self-rising flour = 1 cup all-purpose
   flour plus 1 1/2 teaspoons baking
   powder plus 1/2 teaspoon salt
   (If substituting self-rising flour for
   recipe, omit salt and baking powder
   in recipe.)

1 tablespoon cornstarch =
   2 tablespoons all-purpose flour

1 teaspoon baking powder =
   1 teaspoon baking soda plus
   1/2 teaspoon cream of tartar

1 medium clove garlic = 1/8 teaspoon
   garlic powder or 1/4 teaspoon
   instant minced garlic

1 tablespoon prepared mustard =
   1 teaspoon dry ground mustard

2 cups tomato sauce = 3/4 cup tomato
   paste plus 1 cup water